MATH STUFF

MATH STUFF

The Elements of Curriculum Reform

▼

William N. Bailey

Writers Club Press
San Jose New York Lincoln Shanghai

Math Stuff
The Elements of Curriculum Reform

Writers Club Press
an imprint of iUniverse.com, Inc.

For information address:
iUniverse.com, Inc.
5220 S 16th, Ste. 200
Lincoln, NE 68512
www.iuniverse.com

ISBN: 0-595-14903-0

Printed in the United States of America

To my wife, Jean,
And all the other teachers in my family,
Sarah, Tad, and Ty.

CONTENTS

Recess songs from memory and from The Lore & Language of Schoolchildren by Iona & Peter Opie, ClarendonPress (1959), Oxford Paperbacks (1967).

Preface

Among parents and students, math is often a maligned, misunderstood, and dreaded subject. In cultures that do not appreciate the purpose and importance of a particular subject, development of that field of study on the general level may be seriously impeded. Sadly, such seems to be the case in the United States. American students have scored abysmally low both on the Second and the Third International Math and Science Study, as well as on nationally constructed and administered tests in mathematics. This, I believe, is not just a reflection of an apathy students may have developed toward math or of certain inadequacies of our public school system or of poor teaching. It is also a reflection of a national malaise about studying and learning mathematics, particularly high school math.

Efforts to alleviate and improve this situation have taken many forms including new integrated programs, textbooks, teaching materials, and instructional methods for use in the classroom. Beyond the school, motivational books, mostly dealing with arithmetic, have been written to show that math can be either easy or fun or both. These attempts are targeting immediate changes in student interest and achievement in mathematics.

The approach to the problem advanced in *Math Stuff* is more systemic than cosmetic. It is not about textbook math and therefore contains no equations to solve or theorems to prove. It is, rather, about the nature of this misunderstood subject and the many forces that influence the lesson plan. For example, topics include an historical basis for the math we teach, the political and commercial forces that affect the math program, and some of the provocative and challenging theories on intelligence and learning that are emerging. Of particular importance to the message of *Math Stuff* is the multilevel, almost cubistic portrait of the teacher of mathematics that unfolds. To understand the ideal teacher is a clue to a better understanding of mathematics.

Math Stuff: The Elements of Curriculum Reform does not tell the reader what to think but rather, what to think about. It is written for parents and teachers who want to see beyond the last report card and need to form an answer of their own for that inevitable question, "When will I ever use this stuff?"

APOLOGY

I feel that I must offer an apology for my wanton use of fictitious characters in this otherwise nonfictitious book. However, the term nonfiction, saying more about what a book isn't than what it is, does seem to give me a little slack as to how I choose to classify *Math Stuff*. Actually, the use of fiction to make reality more acceptable and memorable isn't a novel idea. All those nice stories about John painting a fence in three hours and someone known only as A rowing upstream and the guy who wanted to know how high his 20 foot ladder would reach up on the side of a building aren't really true. Yet, who would call an Elementary Algebra book fiction?

Fiction and nonfiction are often thought of in terms of make-believe and reality. Rock-solid, seeing-is-believing, the-real-thing reality, however, has taken some hits from science. Werner Heisenberg, the quantum physicist, said in his uncertainty principle that an observer may alter, even create that which he sees, (or thinks he sees). So, according to the theory, the observer may see a make-believe reality. Not only that but the

Danish scientist , Tor Norretranders believes that of the millions of bits of information that reach our senses in any given moment, only a tiny fraction become part of our awareness. From this minimal amount, the brain constructs a simulated model which we mistakenly interpret as reality. Things being what they appear to be, I don't think the nonfiction—reality connection is wholly reliable.

Perhaps the distinction between fiction and nonfiction would be more appropriately defined in terms of the subject and not the medium. Using art and photography as stand-ins for fiction and nonfiction, I suspect Cezanne and Rembrandt say far more about their subjects than any photographer could while photographs of an exploding star taken from the Hubble telescope have no artistic equivalent. When is the standard for reality composition of meaningful detail and when is it completness of available data? This, it seems to me, depends on what is being viewed?

Math Stuff is looking at the situation in America regarding the teaching and learning of mathematical concepts. Like math itself, the situation is not entirely about solving problems for which there are always answers of which some are right and the others wrong. Perhaps, as chaos theory might suggest, a resolution will emerge from its own data, on its own terms. The style used is intended to be an artistic composition of real data. Viewing the situation through several make-believe eyes, hopefully creates a multidimensional image, an account not of imitation but of conception.

William Bailey
Virginia Beach, Virginia
July 2000

PART I

▼

YOURSELF

When, in your home, around the kitchen table, between TV commercials, in normal conversation, the word "stuff" is used interchangeably with math, you better start thinking about an appointment with the math teacher. The classic question, "When will I ever use this stuff?" deserves serious attention. Stuff is vague. Math is well defined. Stuff is lawless and rootless. Math is logical and axiomatic. There is no future in studying stuff. It's not in the curriculum. It's not on the test.

"When will I ever use this stuff?" When taken at face value, this question presupposes the possibility of a time in the future when, in fact, the math stuff will actually be applicable to some specific task for a particular purpose. More than likely, however, the question is an expression of total frustration and/or boredom in the immediate rather than a speculative concern about the future. Either way, you've got a problem and a heart to heart with the math teacher is indicated.

At such times, it is good to know that, historically, math stuff generally refers to either the subject of the day's lesson, the questions on yesterday's quiz, (returned today), or the even numbered problems 16-60 on page 372 assigned for tomorrow. (Answers to *odd numbered problems only* given at the back of the text.) Specifically, math stuff could be taken to mean:

> If, in two triangles, two angles and a side of one are congruent respectively to two angles and a side of the other, then the triangles are congruent.... If John can cut the grass in two hours and Jim can do it in three hours, how long would it take to cut the grass if John and Jim worked together?....Find the sixth term of the expanded binomial $(2a-3b)^{10}$.... One bag contains three red marbles and five green marbles. A second bag contains six red and two green marbles. If two marbles are drawn, one from each bag, what is the probability that they will be the same color?....

Stuff like that. So, when will your son ever use that stuff? One perfectly straight answer you could try, but of little relevance, is that you used it 30-some years ago when you were in high school.

Maybe temporary familiarity with math stuff assisted you in satisfying requirements for a high school diploma and got you into college, or set you up for a good job, or perhaps broadened your social opportunities. Having done whatever it did, you'll have to admit, occasions to use Heron's Formula or DeMoivre's Theorem simply haven't come up lately. Not to feel too badly about that though because there is, in fact, only one job that can absolutely guarantee the everyday use of math stuff. That job, of course, is teaching high school mathematics which makes it a pretty unique profession. I mean, you don't have to be an English teacher to read The Red Badge of Courage or a biology teacher to talk about fruit flies but who besides a math teacher would set up a two column proof?

Daily use of Pythagorean identities is one dead give-away of a math teacher. Somewhere in a crowded room you hear "Verify $\sin \phi \ (1 + \cot^2 \phi) = \csc \phi$," and bingo! a math teacher. There are other ominous clues such as the cavalier use of ! as in 6! or "i" as not in "inept" but rather as in $2i\sqrt{3}$. It is best not to dwell on these little idiosyncrasies with your child and certainly not draw attention to them with the teacher. After all, most math teachers were brought up through the same sequential, "algeometrig" system that now frames Johnny's perceptions. They are primed to accept the immutable order and the deductive truths inherent in their field along with its special language and weird symbols. That they alone use math stuff daily only adds to the importance and extent of their teaching duties and their public mission. Meeting awesome responsibilities requires that they be skilled, demanding, and informed. Since, in the opinion of the school administration, Johnny's math teacher is skilled, demanding, and informed, he is, ergo, meeting his full responsibilities (Law of Detachment). For the sake of a successful interview, assume this is a given.

The teacher's responsibility is not just to know math. It is also to know how to teach math and, as you may recall from your own high school days back in good old SHS, that could be pretty tricky. Remember your algebra class? For instance, at no time did Oldladydavis allow doubts to sneak in about the lasting practicality of factoring the difference of two squares. Nor did she concede openly that mixing tea at 60 cents a pound with cheap 40 cent tea was indeed a waste of good tea as well as the making of a stupid problem. And all of you who ever paddled a canoe were convinced that, at some point in real time, you would have to paddle upstream to B and back downstream to A to determine the rate of speed of your canoe in still water. Somehow, Oldladydavis made everything seem real or possible and the word stuff in its present usage never came up. But then, that was before the shock waves of the great awakening of the 60's and 70's reached SHS or any of the other high schools.

Research on the subject is scant but it is generally agreed that common use of the word stuff as a generic replacement for math in high schools first appeared during the counter culture revolution inspired by Woodstock and fueled by the anti-authority sentiments of the Vietnam era. The "Hell no, we won't go" chanted on college campuses also sparked discord at the secondary level. Since most of the pre-draft age young men weren't about to go anywhere yet, they focused their ire at what they had to do in the meantime. Clearly in their uncertain futures, they saw no use and little meaning for the extra-neous roots of some hypothetical radical equation. Pointless and boring to the max. I mean, like, you know,...stuff!

The down the road fall out of all that was a great effort on the part of the textbook people to make math relevant and if not that, at least "exciting." Instead of riding on trolley cars from A to B, the students flew jets. Triangulations involved exotic vertices and distances, cer-tainly not rowboats, kite strings, or tree shadows. The real key to making math exciting, however, was brevity. A var-ied menu of mini courses evolved where students could design their own meal tickets to graduation. From the teachers' point of view, the unique advantages of this pro-gram were, a mini course was too brief to be boring and even if it was boring, it was the student's fault for selecting it in the first place (logical consequences).

All this history is important to know before you see the math teacher. In time, high schools went back to full year courses. Some could be taken in two parts but the whole course is what earned the credit. Today, mini courses, by whatever name, will not be seriously considered as a possi-ble solution to the math stuff problem so don't bring them up. Anyway, like it or not, schools are now into the "stan-dards" thing.

According to the papers and the politicians and all those people far from the action in an algebra classroom, every student today will have to "master" algebra before they are let out. By master, they don't really mean master like maybe Newton did. They mean that kids all over the country will have to learn 100 or 200 or 317, whatever, very specific formulas or processes and then all take the same test on the same day on those very same things and then get at least 70% of them correct. in order to achieve a *Master of Algebra* credit. Standards, they say, will provide the means for establishing accountability for students, teachers, and programs. Teaching will be done on a business like basis. With a clearly detailed job description and a standardized product to hustle, teachers will have no room for error much less creativity. Each student's 70% success curve will be routinely monitored to achieve the desired result. Teachers will sell and students will buy. Promotions and hype will be produced as needed to win over the necessary constituencies. It's a sure thing…. But will the "standards" de-stuff math? Remember to ask the math teacher about this.

You might also ask about where to place the emphasis in Johnny's question, "When will I ever use this stuff?" What is the question in his question? Typically, a point in time is sought as an answer. Math classes aren't designed to speculate on the *whens* in a student's life. Think of the useless answers' the math teacher could throw out to a tenth grader. "When you become an engineer…. When you become a rocket scientist…. When you become a statistician, an investment broker…. When you become, ta-dah, a math teacher?" About the only certain answer a math teacher could give to a tenth grader is, "When you become an eleventh grader." *When* is a good question but math teachers can't answer it.

Try *how*. *How* will the stuff be used is another option, partly covered by *when*, but not entirely. *How* could get you into areas ranging from logic and analysis to brain aerobics. Again, not included in the traditional algebra syllabus. Without meaningful responses to *when* and *how*,

Johnny's question would seem to have no plausible answer much less offer a clue as to how to de-stuff math.

Unless! Unless the key word in Johnny's question is *this*. Pronouns can stand for many things. There is a window of hope here. *This* could, of course, refer specifically to *what* stuff is being studied, the sines, radicals, quadratics, and stuff. That would be too obvious. How about, then, *whose* stuff? Clearly, the effectiveness of Johnny's listening skills is a function of who is talking. Some people get all-ears attention all the time. Words of others can fall on deaf ears. That *who* is a factor seems to be quite evident. Now, what would this mean to the de-stuffing problem? Who is *who*? and "When will Johnny ever use *whose* stuff? Another goody for the math teacher.

On the third day after the first outburst of the month of "I hate math!" with the usual references to "this math stuff," you make your move. Armed with up-dated background information and some specific questions, you set out for the high school. Walking to school as before, that old innate sense of unpreparedness kicks in. Undiminished horror nearly stops you in your tracks as you recall those oral French phonetics tests. But today you are an empowered parent. So, keep thinking math. Warmed and reassured by visions of Oldladydavis making math magically clear and believable to the whole class with just three pencils (lines) between the fingers of her hand (plane) almost touching (intersecting) somewhere (point) before transfixed eyes, you recall with some sense of pride that though you never used the concept outright, you have, in fact, never forgotten Oldladydavis's polyhedral angle. With renewed confidence, buoyed by this reminiscence, you boldly approach the MAIN ENTRANCE.

There are six solid, windowless green doors. All business, you yank assertively the colorless handle of the first door on the left. A sudden reverse-impact shock in your right shoulder painfully tells you that the door is either locked or it isn't a door. More gentle trials at the second, third, and fourth doors tell the same story. Betting now on door number six, you nevertheless feel obligated to have a go at five. An abrupt thump interrupts you. The second door swings violently to its maximum open position. A rather small boy rushes out, not seeing you, not looking back, free at last, runs. The scene fills your imagination with possible causes and effects, means and ends, actions and reactions. Reversing the flight of the young boy, you are well through door five and halfway down the ENTRANCE HALL, forgetting your bet on the sixth door.

Before you is a long, glass trophy case filled with shiny cups and bowls, an aging and deflated football and the limp remains of a basketball net. There are fading yellow and red pompoms and plaques and dozens of those towering, gaudy, plastic interpretations of classical Olympian triumph. *We are number one.*

This is the MAIN HALL. On your left is a large room with glass windows and doors that open both on the ENTRANCE HALL and the MAIN HALL. On each is printed OFFICE. A yellow cardboard sign scotch taped on the inside of the corner window says in red letters ALL VISITORS MUST SIGN IN. Ceiling florescent light brightly fills the room and spills through the hall windows into the now darkening MAIN HALL. *We have nothing to hide here. Have a nice day.*

A rather short, post middle aged woman is working at one of the four desks in the room. The other three desks are empty and their surfaces cleared. "Can I help you," she says moving to the high counter which unmistakably divides the room into two domains, staff and student, official and unofficial, haves and have nots. You have the distinct feeling that she fully expects you to ask if this is where you pay your electric bill and then she can send you off to get whatever you don't have or do whatever you haven't done but need to do. Instead, smiling, she reaches under the counter, pulls out a VISITORS SIGN-IN BOOK, finds the current page and (her only intimidating gesture), asks if you have a pen. You flash your trusty scripto and write your name under NAME and 3:25 under TIME IN. Having successfully passed that test, you ask where you might find the math teacher. You hastily qualify that by adding your *son's* math teacher...math, algebra and whatever...trig or something...the tenth grade course. While you are working your way through this verbal confusion, the rather short lady has noticed your name, found your son's file, printed your name on a VISITORS PASS, and then, on a small piece of paper, writes 407. "That's Mr. Brill's classroom. You can go out that door, turn left and walk to the end. Take a right and the first hall you come to is the 400 HALL. Mr. Brill's room will be on your left." You stick the VISITORS PASS on the left side of your jacket, pat it protectively as if to show the nice lady that you respect the rules, say thank you, and head out on your mission.

At the end of MAIN HALL is the cafeteria, still smelling of French Fries so heavily that it is impossible to detect what else, if anything, was served. You turn at the

400 HALL and note on your left 401, 403, 405, and 407. For a moment, you stand in the open doorway. A teacher, obviously a math teacher, is erasing -ocus (3,5) and directr—y = 3 and——abola. Momentarily spared the eraser by your sudden appearance, the equation $(x—3)^2 = 4(y—4)$ stands alone. Breaking the silence, you ask, "How can you de-stuff math."

"Like this," says the math teacher, smiling as he erases $(x—3)^2 = 4(y—4)$ with feigned vengeance. "Good question, whatever it's asking. I'm Tom Brill."

RECESS
London's burning,
London's burning,
Fetch the engines,
Fetch the engines,
Fire, fire!
Fire, fire!
Pour on water,
Pour on water.

PART 2

▼

TOM BRILL

Shaking hands, you introduce yourself as Johnny's dad. "That stuff," you say pointing to the erased remnants of the parabola. "You know, the old question about using this stuff. It's not the stuff that bothers me. It's thinking of math as stuff. Maybe if math wasn't regarded as stuff, students would find their own use for it."

Mr. Brill is overwhelmed by the suddenness and magnitude of your remarks. There is obviously a depth here, a complexity for which, at the end of a school day, he isn't fully prepared. Buying time to get his thoughts in line, Mr. Brill pulls over one of the student's desks so it faces the oak

front of his and gestures for you to have a seat. Without
thinking about the consequences, you politely squeeze
between the hard straight back of the desk and it's
unyielding, vice-like writing surface. You hear a pencil
snap somewhere in the inside pocket of your jacket as you
lean forward and your check book, forced up by the sudden pinch, spills out on the desk top. You are somewhat
relieved to find that by sitting erect, you can gain a half
inch of tummy space.

By comparison Mr. Brill, whose 30 inch waist creates
the impression that he is at least six foot three and not five
eleven, seemingly glides into his free standing, oak desk
chair with plenty of room to spare. He looks to be fresh
out of college or graduate school. His shiny black hair
already shows signs of receding and a narrow chin leaves
his mouth in a permanent whistling mode. Other than
that, the blue oxford cloth button down shirt, the striped
tie, and the blue blazer hanging on his chair behind him
tell the rest, except for the high probability, yet to be confirmed, of loafers concealed by the desk.

Looking straight at you, you half expect to hear Yankee
Doodle but instead hear, "I'm Tom. This is my first year of
teaching. I've got to tell you, I love it but I'm pretty naive
about what should be changed and how changes come
about. I teach what is in the syllabus and use the textbooks
they give me. I know what you mean about stuff but I'm
not sure I can help you."

"Maybe that's good," you say. "We're both new at this.
I'll start where you are."

You think of the two questions you were going to ask.
You reject the one about standards and move on to the one
about whose stuff. "Kids pay attention to certain people,"

you say. "Perhaps we could bring out the people in math, the ones who talked about parabolas and quadratics. What do you think?"

"I think I can help you with the history but I'm not sure about the people part," he says somewhat relieved and turns to the bookcase beside his desk. You see Johnny's textbook and a couple of other hardbacks. By their titles, you judge these must be his college texts. In addition, there are several well used three ring binders each filled with class notes. He pulls one of them out, places it on his desk. Then he reaches back and pulls out Johnny's text and starts turning pages.

"Let's see, Descartes Rules for Signs, De Moivre's Theorem, Horner's Method, Cramer's Rule, Pascal's Triangle, the Pythagorean Theorem, Heron's Formula and, of course, there's always Newton and Kepler. Let's see...."

"If they are the people the kids will listen to. What did they say.?" you ask.

Still talking to himself, Mr. Brill goes on..."well, actually, most of the math taught in high schools today is Cartesian-Newtonian math."

"What happened to algebra?" you say, then add tentatively, "and polyhedral angles?"

"For that matter, most of the math taught in schools for the past 300 years is Cartesian-Newtonian math. That is, the math we have been teaching and still teach follows from the math developed by Descartes and Newton."

"Newton? What did he say?"

"Newton followed Descartes by about 40 or 50 years in the 17th century. Descartes was in the first half, more or less, and Newton did most of his work in the second half.

There wasn't even a Harvard when Descartes started arithmeticizing geometry."

"Doing what to it?"

"Assigning numbers to points and distances and displaying these on a plane. You know, graphing...x-axis...y-axis, that sort of thing. Descartes invented a way to analyze geometry numerically. A line was still a line but it had a quantitative direction and contained unique and numerically identifiable points. Those who followed Descartes greatly refined his method, establishing the rectangular coordinate, or Cartesian plane as we know it where each point is given an ordered pair of numbers. That equation I just erased as you came in defined a unique set of points on a Cartesian plane which formed a special line, a curved line, called a parabola. When broken down, the equation can tell everything about the curve without having to graph it, look at it, that is. In other words, the parabola can be analyzed in terms of its numerically expressed properties.

"That's what Descartes did. What did he say?"

"What he said and demonstrated was that the calculations of arithmetic and algebra are related to the operations of geometry. For example, he would solve quadratic equations geometrically. Anyway, eventually all this led to analytic geometry which is included in our algebra courses. Ask Johnny about slopes and intercepts and distance and stuff, I mean properties, like that.

You are not comfortable with this and say, "What I am looking for is what writers and publishers call the hook."

Mr. Brill gets up and starts pacing in front of the blackboard. "Something simple," he says, "something simple but seen in a new light. How about this for starters? The Greeks thought of x^2 as area and x^3 as volume. Descartes thought of them as lines. Likewise, lines for x^4, x^5, or x^n for that matter. How's that?"

"It has possibilities," you say.

"If y is the area of a square x by x, then the area of that square can be represented by that line we called a parabola, area as a line, you see," he said gracefully coiling down once again into his chair.

You don't need this scene to remind you of the shrinking desk phenomenon you are experiencing. You are barely able to get out the words, "You lost me."

"What did Newton say? He said, 'If I have seen farther than Descartes, it is because I have stood on the shoulders of giants.' This might get us into earlier mathematicians. How about that?"

"Go for it," you say, "but keep it simple. You know, the hook thing. And make it quick. This desk is in its final stage of closure." You turn and, putting one hand on the back of the desk and the other on the writing surface, you bench press your way to freedom. Somewhere in the back of the room, Mr. Brill finds an old bentwood chair with a round seat. "Thanks Tom," you say appreciatively, with the emphasis on Tom. Being well trained at good old SHS in the art of setting up the auditorium with bentwood chairs, you casually spin this one on its left rear leg so it faces Tom's desk. Lacking the figure to execute the difficult coiling maneuver, however, you simple sit. "As you were saying."

"We could start with Thales," he said, leafing through his college notes. "We're talking 585 BC. Let's see...Thales...base angles of an isosceles triangle are equal...vertical angles are equal...congruent triangles...."

Almost 2600 years later and that is still the basis of our geometry course."

"I had something earlier in mind," you say.

"Right! Egypt...3000 BC...Hieroglyphic numerals...areas...quadratics...Basic linear algebra...Ahmes Papyrus....Babylonia...cuneiform records...1900—1600 BC...cubic equations...polygonal areas...Pythagorean Theorem...that's a good 1000 years before Pythagoras, by the way...."

"Joking. Do we have to go all the way back to the beginning?"

"My fault," Tom says, "I tend to be linear. But it might be fun knowing that if Columbus had read Parmenides, 450 BC, he wouldn't have worried about sailing off the edge of the earth, as the myth goes."

"The hook," you remind him.

"There was this one Greek mathematician, Apollonius of Perga, who lived around 200 BC. He wrote a book, eight actually, in which he fully described conic sections including even analytic definitions with references to fixed points and foci. The books were virtually unread for nearly 2000 years when Kepler found them. The result was the laws of planetary motion were completely rewritten. One wonders if Ptolemy would have spent so much thought on his planetary system of cycles and epicycles had he read Apollonius's books. It pays to keep up, you know."

"I'm trying to," you say.

"All right, how about how algebra got its name?" Before you can comment, Tom races on. "From the title of a book called Al Jabr Wa'l Muqabalah. It was written in the early 800's by one of the greatest mathematicians of

the time, Al-Khowarizmi, which is where the word algo-
rithm comes from incidentally."

You can tell, Tom is beginning to enjoy this. Looking
pointedly at your wrist watch is a clue totally wasted.
"Anybody write any jokes back then? Math jokes?"

Tom reads; How many pairs of rabbits will be produced
in a year, beginning with a single pair, if in every month
each pair bears a new pair which becomes productive from
the second month on?

"That's more of a riddle than a joke," Tom adds, "but it
produces one of the most intriguing sequences known."
Tom gets up and writes on the board 1, 1, 2, 3, 5, 8, 13,
21,…. "Each new term of the sequence is the sum of the
two preceding terms."

"So?"

"So its the famous Fibonacci sequence?"

Obviously, Tom is now playing with you. You have a
sense of being hooked. "All right," you say, "what's the deal
on the Fibernasty sequence?"

"Leonardo of Pisa (1180—1250), better known as
Fibonacci, was the son of an Italian merchant. He traveled
throughout the Mediterranean world, much of it in
Greece, Egypt, and Syria, and became quite knowledgeable about the methods of Arabic algebra. Just as Marco
Polo and others brought back tea and spices to western
Europe, Fibonacci brought back Hindu-Arabic numerals,
including zephirum, the sign 0, or as we call it zero or
cipher. Though he aligned algebra with geometry, showing
that they were related and support each other, his greatest
concern was the number. No wonder! He may have been
one of the first to use zero but nobody used the + and -
signs until 1489 or the decimal point until 1492 and the

notations that were used for fractions would make real believers of the 'math is stuff' cult."

"His sequence, the rabbits. Where is the element of surprise, the climax, the mathematicians a-ha?

Tom gets up and adds to the sequence on the board.... 34, 55, 89, 144,.... "Now," he says, returning to his desk and scanning his notebook, "Now...a-ha, here. Ready for this? In most flowers, the number of petals is one of those numbers except the 144. In the head of a sunflower, the little florets appear in two sets of spirals. In one set the spirals go in a clockwise direction and in the other, the direction is counter-clockwise. Pairing the number of spirals in the clockwise set with the number in the counter-clockwise set, the numbers are often 34 and 55. Sometimes they are 89 and 144. Consecutive Fibonacci numbers. Also it has been noted that leaves growing on a branch occur at distances from one another that conform to the sequence numbers. And, do you know what else?" Tom asked triumphantly.

"The number of sticks in a beaver's dam are invariably Fibonacci numbers?"

"I'll have to check that," he says, "but any member of the sequence divided by the number after of it yields a close approximation of the golden ratio. The farther out you go on the sequence, the larger the numbers, the closer is the approximation."

"Right! What's the golden ratio?"

"About .6180338," Tom says, reading his notes.

"Just as I thought," you quip.

"Actually, there is a special rectangle that can be easily constructed with a compass and straightedge. The ratio of its height to its width is the golden ratio. The front of the Parthenon in Athens is such a rectangle.

"The golden rectangle?" you whisper reverently.

"Exactly, and you know those proportions turn up in paintings of Da Vinci and other famous artists. I am told that they also appear in the lengths of parts in certain musical compositions. In a less aesthetic sense, the golden ratio emerges in the radius of convergence of some power series and…"

"The point is," you say rather forcefully.

"The point is Fibonacci started something. He started people thinking algebraically, enough to keep them busy for a couple hundred years until the real renaissance in math began. Undoubtedly, his sequence had far more connections than he ever imagined but it has provided fun and amazement for centuries." Tom thought for a minute then said, "Maybe that's the key to this de-stuffing math problem. There is something fascinating about being at the point of origin, the starting gate, where it all begins."

He opens Johnny's textbook and randomly examines the content as if for the first time. He flips through page after page, at first slowly then with increasing impatience. "I'm looking for starting points," he says. "My general impression is that this is all work in progress until the very end, the 'answers' section, then it is work completed. No beginning."

"You can't expect everybody to go back to Thales or Al Jabr or whatever every time you start a new chapter, can you?"

"There are many starting points in the history of mathematics. Someday I will have a math 'time-line' with cross references to other events on the front of the classroom above the board. I will highlight starting points and talk about them as they became relevant to course material."

"Back up. What's so great about starting points?"

"I think of starting points as the moment between a realized need and a solution," he says.

"If I remember correctly," you venture, "some starting points can be hazardous to your health."

"It is said that the Pythagoreans killed one of their members for fear he would divulge the existence of irrational numbers."

"Didn't Galileo and Copernicus get into trouble with the church over some of their new ideas?"

"You can bet," Tom says, "they will both be up there on my time-line along with Regiomontanus, Briggs, Harriot, Napier, and Kepler. Napier invented logarithms, you know, and Kepler, with that major assist from Apollonius, developed further laws about conics and the paths of planets and their satellites."

Oldladydavis comes through again. That plastic cone on her desk with the colored sections flashes through your mine. "You mean circles and parabolas and ellipses," you say with mock confidence.

"And hyperbolas," Tom adds.

"You will definitely need a bigger wall."

Tom looks up and, framing a portion of the wall with his hands, says, "Right there, Francois Viete (1540—1603). Now there's someone who really started something like moving math out of the Renaissance into the modern age."

"Sixteenth Century, the modern age? Now we're getting somewhere."

"All right, up to now Arabic algebra had been worked to its limits. Third degree or cubic equations had been

solved along with quartic equations. Trigonometry was
recognized as a discipline of its own. The problem was, the
notations used, the symbols, were sufficiently useful to
apply to specific situations but lacked the flexibility to
develop broad algebraic generalities. Viete, who wasn't a
mathematician by the way, he was a lawyer, introduced the
idea of using letters for variables and constants He trans-
formed algebra and trigonometry into literal subjects. As
such, generalized formulas or "laws" could be derived. He
showed the relationship between the roots and the coefi-
cients of an equation. In trig, he came up with a law of
tangents for oblique triangles plus several others involving
multiple angles. In other words, Viete uncorked the bottle.
Mathematics was free to go.

"It took a lawyer, huh? Maybe lawyers could design a
stuff-less curriculum."

"You joke," Tom says, " but I've got another one.
With the powers of new symbols, we jump from simple
equations to the integrals developed by Cavalieri and
Fermat." Again, framing another imaginary rectangle on
the wall, Tom says, "Pierre de Fermat (1601—1665). He
too was a lawyer.

"I rest my case."

"Some people referred to him as 'the prince of
amateurs' but he was hardly that. The man was into
differentiation and integration, maximum and minimum
points, tangents to curves, actually basic calculus, before
Newton was born...60 years before Newton published his
famous 'Principia' in which the calculus as we know it was
introduced. Fermat further advanced number theory,
analytic geometry, and infinitesimal analysis. Often in his
proofs he used reasoning somewhat kin to one of Zeno's

paradoxes like the one about Achilles racing the tortoise. Achilles, it is said, can never overtake the tortoise because as Achilles reaches the tortoise's starting point, the tortoise has advanced some distance and when Achilles covers that distance, the tortoise has moved yet another distance and so on. By this method of infinite subdivision, Achilles can't win the race. Fermat called his method infinite descent and, mathematically, the conclusions were definitely not paradoxical."

"Fermat, eh! Fermat as in Fermat's last theorem? That wasn't another one of those rabbit riddles was it?"

"No! Only in the sense that it kept math people busy for a long time, about 360 years as a matter of fact. You know the Pythagorean Theorem states that the sum of the squares of the sides of a right triangle is equal to the square of the hypotenuse. In symbols, its $A^2 + b^2 = c^2$. Well, Fermat said that it is impossible to separate any power except a square into two powers with the same exponent, meaning the Pythagorean relationship won't work for any exponent greater than 2. It was said that he wrote a proof for his theorem in the margin of a book. Maybe so but it was never found nor was any proof accepted until 1993 when Andrew Wiles presented his 200 page proof.

"You mean for 360 years people worked on that one problem. Was it important? Did it lead to the theory of relativity or DNA or quantum physics or something of that sort?

"Not really," Tom says. "I guess it just stood there like a mathematicians Mount Everest. Over the years it challenged the best of minds. Prizes were offered. Many attempts were made. I guess the simplicity of the theorem lured people on expecting to find a simple proof."

You recall doing geometric constructions with Oldladydavis. Using a straightedge and compass you found midpoints and constructed perpendiculars and you bisected angles, all with great ease. "Don't waste your time trying to trisect an angle." she said, "It can't be done." That did it. You and every other kid in the class were hooked and immediately started to waste your time; maybe not 360 years but hours of time. Giving Tom a knowing look you say, "I can appreciate that."

"Newton," Tom blurts out suddenly.

You counter in kind with, "And Viete."

"Your going the wrong way," he says. "Try Leibniz."

"All right then, Leibniz. Newton and Leibniz. So?"

"Sir," Tom says. "Sir Isaac Newton, if you please, and Gottfried Wilhelm Leibniz are generally credited with creating, independently of each other, the complete version of the calculus. Viete, Fermat, and others had worked with differentiation and integration in limited and specific ways. Newton and Leibniz were able to generalize the concepts and unify both branches of calculus in the famous fundamental theorem of calculus."

All this is taking too long but you are finding in Mr. Brill a sharp mind and a subtle sense of humor that appeals to you. Only three more centuries to go, you decide to hang in there. "What's the difference between algebra and calculus?" you ask.

"What a great student you would make," Tom says. "You ask all the right leading questions. Algebra is like a snap shot whereas calculus is a moving picture. Calculus is the mathematics of continual change, the mathematics for motion, acceleration, forces, and orbits. We have Newton's first and second laws of motion...a body set in motion tends to remain in motion until acted upon by some external force and the good old F = ma of your physics class; force equals the product of mass and acceleration.... Also, there is the inverse square law or Newton's Law of Gravitation. The mathematical analysis of continuous motion or, in general, change is all made possible because of calculus."

The thought of motion makes you think of that canoe in Oldladydavis's class. "Is Newton's motion anything like the distance-equals-rate-times-time motion, you know like up-stream/down stream or train A goes east while train B goes west sort of motion?"

"Solve your D = RT equation for R and try to find your rate at some given instant. Distance divided by time is meaningless if time T = 0 because division by zero is meaningless. You can't do it. Therefore instantaneous velocity is impossible to determine, right?"

"Wrong! I can read it on my speedometer. 50 miles per hour right...now.

"Of course. Mathematically, Newton allowed that the intervals of time on either side of zero to get smaller and smaller as they 'approached' zero time. The 'limit' of the change in distance divided by the change in time, your D over T, as the time change gets continually close to zero, but never hits it, is the instantaneous R or velocity." Tom looks at you almost apologetically and then says quickly as if to sneak it by you, "He also invented the binomial theorem."

"Moving right along."

"Johann Sebastian Bach."

"I beg your pardon."

Looking at his notes Tom reads, "The Bach of math was the Swiss mathematician Leonhard Euler (1707–1783). Let's see...both had a wide range of interests...both produced large families...for Euler, 13 children...both were prolific writers...neither spent much time revising his work but rather moved on to write something new...while Bach could write a sonata before breakfast, Euler could write mathematical articles while playing with his children...both developed serious eye problems which rendered them blind in their late years....There has got to be your hook in there somewhere."

"I have to admit," you say, "seeing the human side sort of makes the achievements, the so called stuff, more real too."

"Euler was a serious student of theology, medicine, astronomy, physics, Hebrew, and oriental languages. He wrote in Latin and French even though German was his native language. He wrote well over 500 articles and books, so many the Swiss government created a special fund to collect them all.

"What math did he do in his spare time?"

"Let me count the ways," Tom sings poetically. "Differential equations, topology, complex analysis, an algebra for sets or groups of things like an algebra for whole forests and not just trees or numbers as it had been. He was the first to treat logarithms as exponents as we now teach them. However, his special, almost comical contribution to math was the formula $e^{i\pi} + 1 = 0$ which puts all the special numbers in one equation.

"I'm sure you are holding back something but I'm impressed. Euler, he's my man."

"Wait till you see what we've got coming up in the nineteenth century."

"Nineteenth century, who's the biggy?"

"I've got to go with Gauss," Tom says, but there is also Cauchy, Bolyai, Dedekind, Cantor, Peano, Poincare, and of course...."

"Gauss," you say. "Stick with Gauss."

"OK, but there are some special cases I think you will have to hear about. You know it took 400 years to get from Al-Khwarizmi to Fibonacci and another 375 to get to Viete, then only about 90 more and we reach Newton with Euler not far behind. Talk about acceleration. From here on, math really takes off. I see a quote here I've saved from my course at the university that says it pretty well. Its from our text 'A History of Mathematics' by Boyer and Merzbach.

> The nineteenth century, more than any preceding period, deserves to be known as the Golden Age in mathematics. The additions to the subject during these one hundred years far outweigh the total combined productivity of all preceding ages. The century was also, with the possible exception of the Heroic Age in ancient Greece, the most revolutionary in the history of mathematics. The introduction into the mathematician's repertoire of concepts such as non-Euclidean geometries, n-dimensional spaces, noncommutaive algebras, infinite processes, and nonquantitative structures all contributed to a radical transformation which changed the appearance as well as the definition of mathematics.

The math from here on can be pretty specialized and abstract. I'll stay close to the mathematicians and not the mathematics they produce. OK?'

"I wouldn't want it any other way," you jest and then add, "but I'm not sure whether we are further stuffing or de-stuffing math. Oh what the heck, this is all new to me. I'd just as soon hear about the history of mathematicians as I would the history of Popes and Kings and battles. Who have you got to go with Gauss?"

"First Gauss, Carl Friedrich (1777–1855). Like Euler, he was into many non-math things too such as astronomy, geodesy, electricity and magnetism, and languages. He predicted the precise orbits of comets and the asteroid Ceres. He invented ways of mapping on spheres and curvatures, even negative curvatures. The unit of magnetic induction is called a gauss after guess who."

"You are dying to get to the math, aren't you?"

"He had sadness in his personal life," Tom continued. "His first wife died leaving him with children to care for. He married again but she also died. At first he had trouble getting the recognition he deserved but eventually he assumed an almost superhuman reputation among mathematicians. Often it occurred that a prominent mathematician would publish a new idea only to find later the same idea in some of Gauss's unpublished notes. Mathematicians saught him out for support and assistance. One famous account was of a Monsieur Leblanc who in correspondence greatly impressed Gauss. It turned out that Leblanc was actually Sophie Germain who at that time feared that being a woman would hinder her chances of being accepted as a serious mathematician. Of course, after Gauss praised her work publicly, she was duly recognized."

"I am ready for the math part," you tell him.

"As a teenager, Gauss figured out how to construct a regular polygon of 17 sides with a straightedge and compass. Except for triangles and special cases, little had been done, particularly with polygons having a prime number of sides. Later he developed the Fundamental Theorem of Algebra, advanced the study of number theory, legitimized the complex number, derived formulas for statistics, and further developed elliptic functions. One thing he didn't do. He didn't accept the challenge to prove Fermat's last theorem perhaps because he knew how complex the problem was."

"Did Gauss ever teach?"

"As a matter of fact, he apparently dodged the classroom as much as possible. He managed an observatory and what good students he did have mostly became astronomers. Maybe it was like famous writers not wanting to teach creative writing."

You think for a minute and then say, "My creative writing teacher didn't like to write. She told us she would be a good writer if she only had something to say."

"In math, it is not just saying something. It is saying something to the most brilliant, critical, discerning, proud, at times arrogant, professional audience ever about something new that, nevertheless, fits legitimately into an ageless succession of ideas and logically derived theorems which is continually being extended."

"I would be speechless."

"Consider this," Tom says. "Forever, the vision of space and form was defined for us by the earliest Greek mathematicians. Euclid's postulates were not merely accepted but believed to be true. Recall the one that said if you have a line and a point that is not in the line, then there is only one line that can be drawn parallel to the given line. Obvious as that is, to a 19th century mathematician being obvious is not a condition for validity. Since it was a postulate for which there was no proof, one could just as well postulate alternatives and see what kind of geometry evolves. The Russian mathematician Nickolai Ivanovich Lobachevsky (1793—1856) postulated not one parallel line but many. Accepting Euclids other postulates he invented a new, non-Euclidean geometry which is called hyperbolic geometry. The plane of action was not flat but rather precisely curved. Among other differences that followed, one was that the sum of the angles of a triangle was less than, not equal to 180 degrees. A more dramatic difference was that the measures of Lobachevskian radii and distances were imaginary or complex numbers which led some people to refer to his creation as imaginary geometry. To that critical, discerning audience of mathematicians, Lobachevskian geometry was given little notice. This proved to be so disturbing to him that he gave up his work in mathematics. Today, Lobachevskian geometry is hardly regarded as imaginary in the literal sense. It is critical to our understanding and analysis of outer space. To complete the story, it should be stated the Farkas Bolyai and Gauss also developed a hyperbolic geometry independently of Lobachevsky."

"Euclid said one parallel," you say, "and Lobachevsky said many parallels. Who is going to come up with no parallels?"

"Georg Friedrich Bernhard Riemann (1826–1866), along with Euler and Gauss, he made up the big three of the golden age of 19th century math. In a very simplified way, we can think of lines as 'shortest distances' between two points. On the earth, the shortest distance between two points is along a great circle, like the great circle routes the airlines fly. The parallels of latitude are not great circles, except the equator of course. The meridians of longitude are great circles and they all intersect at the poles. Parallels don't intersect, therefore, on the earth, there are no parallel shortest distances. In terms of curvature, the earth is said to be a positively curved surface. Euclid's plane has zero curvature. Lobachevsky's hyperbolic plane has negative curvature. An example of how all this affects simple geometry, compared to the circumference of a circle on a plane with zero curvature, the circumference of a circle with the same radius is less on positively curved surfaces and greater on negatively curved surfaces. And, on the positively curved surface, the sum of the angles of a triangle is greater than 180 degrees. Riemann's version of non-Euclidean geometry is called elliptical geometry and is on positively curved surfaces. If you care to get into it further, look up his zeta function conjecture and be the first to prove it."

You pretend that you are writing. "That's zeta with a z, isn't it ?"

"Success and recognition does not always come easily to a mathematician as we saw in the case with Lobachevsky. There are two others that faired far worse than he. One was Niels Henrik Abel (1802—1829). At the age of 16 he read Gauss's 'Disquisitiones' and obviously showed great promise as a mathematician. His first misfortune occurred when his father died and he had to leave school to earn money for the family. In time, however, he did earn advanced degrees and, in 1824, published a paper. As with playwrites who seek a good review for approval and fame, Abel sent his paper to Cauchy who lost it. Recognizing its importance, one of Abel's friends urged Cauchy to find the paper. By the time it was found, Abel had died in poverty from tuberculosis. He was 26 years old. Two days after he died, a letter arrived offering him a professorship at the University of Berlin. His work was in group theory, an abstract math which had no practical application and was neither well known nor appreciated at that time. Today, of course, it is highly respected branch of mathematics employing concepts which bear his name, the abelian group and the abelian variety."

Tom respects your silence then continues. "Number two, Evariste Galois (1811–1832). Like Abel, Galois was a brilliant teenager and he too sent papers to Cauchy, twice as a matter of fact, and both times Cauchy threw them away. Bad as this was, it wasn't the worse thing that happened to Galois. As a student, he was much more interested in concepts and theories than he was in details. Exams probably bored him with their emphasis on detailed answers. Twice he failed the entrance exam to the Ecole Polytechnique. About this time his father, who was a mayor and in political difficulty, killed himself. Galois went through a period of being an angry revolutionary, rebelling against the authorities of his school and later rebelling against certain elements of the government. He spent time in jail and for various reasons made enemies who, it is said, tricked him into defending the honor of a coquette in a duel. Throughout the entire night before the duel, he wrote in a letter to a friend new theories and proofs of ideas he had expressed before. Early the next morning, he was killed. Galois was 20 years old. His notes were astounding and took years of study to comprehend. Basically, the Galois Theory makes it possible to move from an infinite set to a finite set, that is one with a finite set of elements."

"Twenty years old! My son Johnny is sixteen and he isn't even up to Viete yet."

"And we aren't up to the twentieth century yet although Riemann did open the door. You see, Riemann had provided new geometric ways to conceive of the universe and twentieth century mathematicians were pretty interested in discovering a general theory of everything, meaning the universe. For example, in his flat, zero curvature model, time progresses and space expands with the galaxies becoming ever further apart; an 'open' universe. An alternative is a universe where both time and space are finite. In this model, based on Riemann's elliptic geometry, space has positive curvature and is considered to be spherical; a 'closed' universe starting with the big bang, expanding, then ultimately contracting in a final crunch. Riemann also suggested a modern version of a hyperbolic, negatively curved, 'open' universe where time and space advance infinitely with no crunch at the end. This led to another alternative, the 'half-open' model in which size is finite but time extends infinitely. This particular model, it turns out, lends itself well to the latest 'string' theories of cosmology. Anyway, the thing to note is that Riemann's mathematics of the mid-1800's was vital to the evolving cosmology of the 20th century. In effect, Riemann replaced the old, rigid concepts of space as being an amorphous void with a mathematical description of space giving it form and dimension."

Tom thinks about this for a minute while you have the sense of being way out on a thin limb. "You know," he says, "the message here to me as a teacher is to try to get the kids to look at things in different ways. It is the new perspective that stimulates creative and adaptive thinking. I read somewhere that Riemann decided to think of space in terms of infinitely many lines instead of points. I wonder if such a simple change in his perspective could have sparked a whole new mathematical and scientific concept of space."

"Is that what some people call a paradigm shift?'

"It must be pretty close to it if its not," Tom says leaning back in his chair. He looks at the open notebook on the desk, leafs through until he finds a particular page, and then says, "Basically, what we teach isgeometry...Euclid...300 BC; factoring quadratics, trigonometry...Viete.. 1591; logarithms...Napier...1594; conic sections...Kepler...1604; roots and coefficients...Harriot...1631; analytic geometry, cartesian coordinate plane...Descartes...1637; binomial theorem andcalculus...Newton...1665;divergentseries...Liebniz ...1700; complex analysis, sets...Euler...1748; complex numbers ... Gauss ... 1 8 0 1 ; n o n - Euclideangeometry...Riemann...1854;matrices...Sylvester...1870;.andprobability...Markov...1899. To be perfectly honest, now that it's almost over, I know very little about 20th century math. You would do better talking to Harvey Roper, our physics teacher.

"I've got too many questions about math to take on physics as well."

"Physics and math sort of got blended after 1900. Max Planck gave a talk on December 14, 1900 which changed everything. He simply noted that when matter absorbs heat energy, light energy is emitted discontinuously. Doesn't sound like such a big deal, does it? Except that up to now, light energy has always been a continuous thing. Newton made that perfectly clear. It couldn't turn itself off and on. However, Einstein and others proved that rather than in a continuous wave, light is carried by photons, a concept which later became known as quanta. With these discoveries and Einstein's general theory of relativity in 1916, the whole Cartesian-Newtonian mechanical view of energy and motion would be forever questioned and qualified. This was the start of quantum mechanics. Einstein set it up but couldn't buy into all of it. Niels Bohr became the leading proponent for quantum theory and he was followed by Louis De Boglie, Erwin Schroedinger, Max Born, Werner Heisenberg, Richard Feynman and just about everyone else. So along with the closed and half-open descriptions of the universe, the mathematicians were also trying generate the math that would accommodate atomic structure with all its subatomic particles. In doing so, they also came up with some very astonishing concepts like Heisenberg's 'Uncertainty Principle' and Kurt Godel's 'Incompleteness Theorem.' As of now, not much of this has filtered down to the high school math syllabus."

"Is that it?" you say, preparing to stand up.

"Well, there were some people trying to put language in the domain of mathematics using logic as the basic operator, people like Hilbert and Russell, but that hit a dead end.

"I hate to bring it up but you haven't mentioned the impact computers have had on math. As a final shot, do you want to handle that now?"

"OK! Fast forward to the end of last and the start of the present century...or should I say millennium. So far, computers have been invaluable to speed up computations, store data, display models of whatever and that sort of thing. They have done our bidding basically as we would have done it, sequentially, one step at a time no matter how quickly taken. The new parallel computers do not process data sequentially. Rather, the information is processed on several levels cooperatively, simultaneously, sometime contradicting, sometimes reinforcing itself. These thinking computers continually adapt to the evolving patterns of data, allowing them to become something that was not programmed by man, to have a life of their own so to speak."

"How can you teach a subject when you don't know what it is or where its going?" you ask. "What do you do, just turn it on and watch?"

"Beats me," Tom says. "There is really not much information coming down to my level about the new evolutionary maths. I've read that some of these so called intermaths bear such titles as genetic algorithms, neural networks, classifier systems, and even artificial life. One that I have played around with is cellular automata. Actually, its not new. It was first introduced by John Von Neumann and Stanislaw Ulam in the 1950's. If you care to see how it works and have some fun with it, I can show you how to play John Conway's Game of Life.

"Does this have anything to do with fractals?"

"Well, yes and no. Both start out with a base of operation. In cellular automata, it is the grid of cells in which to operate. In fractals, it may be a geometric figure. Both have algorithms or production rules to follow over a specified number of cycles. Cellular automata can produce a self-similar image like a fractal. Fractals, however, are capable of simulating the branching of limbs on a tree, the changes in the shapes of clouds, and the seemingly infinite fluctuations in a coastline. Although we have fairly recently developed practical applications for fractal technology, most noticeably special effects for motion pictures, its time-line might start with Pythagorean trees and include the 19th century sets of Cantor, Peano, and Hilbert. A student just beginning to investigate fractals would probably start with the Koch curves and Sierpinski gaskets of the early 20th century. Today, the most outstanding mathematician in this field, considered to be the father of modern fractal geometry, is Benoit Mandelbrot."

There is silence. Mr. Brill stands and you say jokingly, "Can I go now, sir? That was some class but I'm fresh out of questions."

He says, "I enjoyed that, really. I liked studying math history in college and I'm glad I kept my notes. I wonder whether I will still be able to talk this way in five or ten years or will I have yielded my time, my creative time that is, to covering every last topic in that 800 page text."

You suddenly realize that his very animated presentation was heart-felt genuine; that Tom Brill is not only an incredible resource but a believer. He does not want his feeling about the importance of math history to be lost or wasted. You shake hands and move toward the door. Tom goes to the back of the room and slides into one of the desks. Studying the front wall he says, "Not big enough."

You turn and, at great peril, cram yourself into the closest desk. "Make slides," you say. "Cross reference them. Show the lines between Apollonius and Newton, Fibonacci and Gauss, whoever. Play math with them. Let them intersect in curved concept-time."

Tom starts laughing. "I will define my starting points as the intersection of two concept-time line segments on a closed elliptic surface. How about that?"

You escape from the desk. "With math, I think it should be an open hyperbolic surface." Waving you say, "Thanks again."

From the door you hear, "Slides? Right! Hey, I thank you."

RECESS

Multiplication is vexation,
Division is as bad,
The rule of three
Does puzzle me
And practice drives me mad.

PART 3

▼

BOB WILLARD

"Except for Galois and Abel, mathematicians seem to have a pretty good life. Consider young Tom Brill. He probably makes a good salary, gets away from the office, classroom, whatever, by four and how about his Christmas, spring, and summer vacations?" Maybe you should have imagined this a long time ago. Then you remember all those thick books in his bookcase. But there was only one high school textbook and maybe that's all you would need. One book, you could handle that. Tonight you will look at Johnny's copy of Algebra 2 With Trigonometry.

As you pass the ghosts of French fries past, take the second left and walk down the hall to the MAIN OFFICE—ALL VISITORS MUST SIGN IN, you quickly check to see if your HALL PASS is still stuck to your jacket. It is and you decide to leave it there until you get inside, just in case.

The VISITOR'S SIGN-IN BOOK is no longer on the counter and the nice lady isn't visible either. On the far side of the room there are two offices. Keeping with the "We have nothing to hide here" theme, both doors are open. Over one is a sign which says MR. GAGE, PRINCIPAL and over the other door a sign which says MR. WILLARD, VICE-PRINCIPAL.

"Hope I haven't kept you waiting," says an amiable looking black man stepping from under the Principal sign. He seems about your age, perhaps a little shorter. His sharply creased pants have a buckle in the back just below the belt. He is wearing no jacket and his white shirt sleeves are folded back one cuff width.

"Mr. Gage?" you say cheerfully.

"No, I'm Bob Willard but Hi, nice to see you." He pulls out the VISITOR'S SIGN-IN BOOK, reads the name on your VISITOR'S PASS, locates your entry noting the destination then fills in the blank TIME OUT column. "Mr. Brill is a very capable young teacher, " he says. "We are pleased to have him on our faculty. Can I be of any further assistance to you?"

Although it was a perfectly reasonable mistake thinking that the man coming out of the Principal's was, in fact, the Principal you, nevertheless, feel slightly embarrassed for starting the moment off on the wrong foot. You further your uneasiness by coming right out with the stupid comment, "I was talking to Mr. Brill about de-stuffing math. Stuff like that."

Mr. Willard doesn't flinch. "De-stuff math?" He thinks for a minute then says, "That's a good one. As in, when am I going to use this stuff. That stuff, you mean? Right! Got a minute? Come on in."

This appearing more like a summons than an invitation, you follow Mr. Willard under the VICE-PRINCIPAL sign into his office. The deep cushioned vinyl chair without a hammer lock of a desk top looks appealing. It seems to exhale all your concerns as you lower yourself into it. You notice diplomas and certificates on the wall, endorsements in secondary administration and K-12 math, an MEd., an MA in Mathematics, and a recognition for something awarded by the State Board of Education. Impressed, you lean forward slightly and say confidently, "You know, I always wondered what it would be like to be a mathematician."

"Mathematician? I'll tell you one thing," he said laughing, "you won't find any mathematicians around here. We're all teachers and some of us teach Math."

Remembering about those guys Viete and Fermat that Mr. Brill talked about, you quip, "How about lawyers?"

Fortunately Mr. Willard who doesn't get the connection is, nevertheless, able to relate rather proudly that yes, there is one lawyer on the faculty, Mr. Roth who teaches U.S. history and government. Lucky for you there was a Mr. Roth. No telling where that conversation might have gone.

Mr. Willard, "Call me Bob, please," is a very accomplished facilitator. He provides many opportunities for you to speak and brings up issues about which there is agreement. He understands your question and, being a math teacher, puts the problem in the domain of the faculty.

"Why not de-stuff English or even Latin? Why is it always math? The problem you raise," he tells you, "is not the only thing that is unique to the subject of mathematics. Some of my faulty may not agree with this but, I've got to say, teaching math is like no other teaching experience. There is nothing quite like it."

"Really? How so?" you ask, sensing happily that your question might not be so dumb after all. "I mean, teaching is teaching. What makes math so different from teaching history or English? Science uses a lot of math. Why don't you hear I hate science?"

The dialogue that follows is uncomplicated. There is an even amount of give and take yet you clearly suspect that Mr. Willard is moving it toward some enlightening conclusions. Mostly you are learning about math teachers and teaching math, stuff you never thought of before.

What you learn is that there are two kinds of people in the math profession, mathematicians and math teachers. The essential concerns of the pure mathematician working in the realm of abstractions are to develop and test new mathematical theories and explore and analyze their logical implications. Another type of mathematician, the applied mathematician, seeks to find practical uses for these. The math teacher is, of course, responsible for inventing plausible, student friendly yet honest and valid explanations for the mathematics given him to teach. Of greater concern to the teacher are the students in whom she or he must instill an appreciation and understanding of the nature and processes of mathematics if not zeal and flawless skills.

Generally, math people can distinguish between the tasks that mathematicians and math teachers do. To others, that distinction may not be wholly accurate. Often, as in your case, a math teacher is thought of as a mathematician though, perhaps, of a lesser rank. After all, a person studying to become a math teacher follows pretty much the same curriculum up to a point as a person who eventually becomes a mathematician. That is he takes courses that continually ascend in complexity requiring higher and higher order thinking skills. Such skills and knowledge, essential to a mathematician, are not necessarily the skills essential to being an effective math teacher. It might be better if cultivating the skills of an excellent teacher of mathematics were not left to chance or assumed to emerge from a healthy dose of complex variables and stochastic processes.

By comparison, other disciplines prepare their teachers by offering a broader horizontal curriculum which uses, basically, existing thinking skills. English teachers can read and enjoy everything from *Good Night Moon* to *King Lear*. There is no clear boundary beyond which their reading is impossible. Shakespeare and Homer, among the greats, well understood basic thinking skills and in their terms could express profound and durable thoughts. It was not for unawareness of basic thinking skills, however, that Einstein was unable to write in narrative form a popular version of his general theory of relativity. Such is the fortune of mathematicians. They communicate in symbols often about things that don't exist and can't be defined. When their working universe becomes too small or too restrictive, they invent new vocabularies and create new environments like space-time to play out their abstractions. It is no wonder that for the most part, if not for all math teachers, there comes the reality that further readings will become increasingly difficult, obscure, and ultimately out of reach. It would be very depressing for an English teacher to confess that he or she could understand none of the best poems or novels now being written. For the math teacher, however, a comparable event such as curling up by the fire and browsing through Andrew Wile"s proof of Fermat's last theorem would have a zero probability of happening yet with no ill side effects.

Further, the inspiration of a great book or major historical event is readily accessible to teachers and students alike and is, in itself, a source of illumination and motivation. About the only book a math student sees is the text and it is hardly in the class of great books. Making great math books available such as Kepler's *Astronomia Nova*, Newton's *Principia*, Gauss' *Disquisitiones* or even Euclid's *Elements* in a Euclidean geometry class would have minimal instructional value at the high school level and would surely get a zero for motivation and inspiration. Whereas Faulkner and Frost can speak directly to English students, and Jefferson and Churchill to history students, and science books are on the Best Seller lists, in math, basically its all up to old Square Root Sam or Radical Sign Rita down the hall or, in your case, Tom Brill in room 407.

On the same idea, math teachers shouldn't bank on much instructional help from parents. Typically, mothers in the defense of their daughters will declare proudly that they never understood geometry either, like it's a girl thing. Fathers on the other hand, though seemingly good at math, explain things in such weird ways it doesn't pay to ask them for help…no offense. Therefore, when it comes to assists from the field, the math teacher is pretty much on his own.

Aside from having to pursue a vertical rather than a horizontal preparatory curriculum and aside from being solely responsible for offering inspiration and instruction, there is yet another element of teaching math that should bear special consideration. Conceivably, math teaching could be thought of as an unencumbered, direct, mind to mind contact where thought processes must conform to the parameters and postulates of a given universe. The basic activity required of the student is simply to think within certain spatial and conceptual constraints.

The down side of this rigor is, and maybe this is your Johnny's problem, that it can place the student where there is no place to hide. There are no fantasies, no safe harbors or acceptable digressions and very few good excuses to barter. The student is vulnerable. A misstep could be interpreted as disinterest or even low ability. Consequently, a struggling math student may be heard to say, "I hate math" whereas in history or English it is more likely to be "I hate Mr. Chalkdust." In math, the subject is usually held responsible for discomfort and misadventure.

In teaching math therefore, positive verbal communication is important. We talk about this in department meetings. Process, not just answers should be assessed. Math is not simply an all right or all wrong situation as many people including, unfortunately, some math teachers think. Understanding the concepts, not speed of computation, is what the student is trying to demonstrate and what the math teacher must look for. It is easy to find out what the student doesn't know. What the boy or girl does know and building on that is the challenge. Speed without so called "careless" mistakes is one objective but clearly not the primary one. Math teachers particularly should be aware of the personal feelings their subject can evoke, feelings that can lead to a student being turned off of math by not being recognized. Of course, any teacher can say this, history, English, chemistry, whatever, but math teachers better believe it. It is hard to express yourself and say something in the language of mathematics.

There is still another unique property associated with mathematics and mathematics teaching. Math competence, the ability to think clearly and imaginatively about math, comes early in life and may not be a sustainable skill. Many of the great mathematicians did their most creative work early in their careers while they were young. The often unappreciated connection here is that math teachers may have students while they are at their cognitive best as far as math is concerned. Not that there will be a Gauss, Galois, or Godel in the classroom but for whomever and at whatever level he or she may be, this is a critical stage and the math teacher is the primary, if not the only source of support. Making the most of limited opportunities is another special feature of being a math teacher.

It is getting late. You are not thinking even hypothetically about becoming a math teacher any longer. Bob Willard leans forward over his desk. He says half whimsically and in a quiet voice, "You know, I am a math teacher but this office is keeping me out of the classroom. At times I truly wonder whether I was promoted or demoted, professionally speaking. The answer to that depends on whether I am a math teacher or an administrator. When I taught math, I really didn't know about math teachers, what we were just talking about. It didn't occur to me that teaching math had such unique properties and responsibilities. I never dealt with the question about 'using this stuff.' Now I would. Looking back, I don't think my agenda was complete. Perhaps I still have that old desire for closure."

It is your chance to offer advice. "You will find a way to be both a math teacher and an administrator. They are not mutually exclusive. In fact, teachers probably need a teaching teacher in the main office."

"You're right," he says. "I just may take a pre-calculus section next fall. Actually what I would really like to do is write a new course for all those who, having earned their three credits, now want out of math; a course that would tie together all the math they have had and allow them to use it in novel and creative ways."

Mr. Willard starts to add something but then drops it perhaps because it is either too technical or too personal. There is a concluding silence you share and then, rising, you thank him though for precisely what you aren't sure. It was definitely more than a friendly conversation or a spare moment of his time. You walk to the counter. He puts the VISITORS SIGN-BOOK away. You peel off your VISITORS PASS. He holds out his hand and offers to take it. You put it in your pocket instead and shake his hand. "Again, thanks," you say. Smiling, he replies, "De-stuffing math is still on our agenda."

There are now many students in the ENTRANCE HALL, either holding or standing beside black musical instrument cases. They are talking and laughing and barely notice you as you try to thread your way to the doors. You push open the door that the small boy used earlier. Before you are out, you see that same boy excitedly running toward you. For you he triumphantly holds up a black clarinet and greets you with, "I made the band." You stand aside and hold the door as he rushes through.

So much for cause and effect.

RECESS
Teacher, teacher, let me in,
My feet's cauld, my shoes are din.
If ye winna let me in,
I'll no come back in the efternin.

PART 4

▼

REBECCA FEINMAN

Rebecca Feinman owns Oxbow Books, Your favorite neighborhood bookstore. She is overweight, has bad feet, and wears thick glasses. She was a middle school science teacher for thirty years and, shortly after Mr. Feinman died, she sold her house and a lot of stuff, took early retirement, and opened Oxbow Books.

Oxbow is one of those small, one room bookstores that either has exactly what you want or can get it for you in three days max. Its most unusual characteristic, however, is that you can always find a book or journal article that you never heard of before but, on checking it out, realize that it is something you need now. Such is the case today.

"Becky," you say browsing the contemporary drama shelf, "I'm not a teacher and never was but lately I've been getting into their business."

Not looking up from a red covered journal she is reading she comes back with, "You're still an active parent aren't you? They're fair game."

Becky likes to be *immediate* which is slightly ahead of *current.* That's why she stocks and reads journals, not exclusively but mostly pertaining to science, economics, world politics, and education. These she rarely ever sells but is apt to pull one out and announce, "Here's something worth reading." And, of course, it always is. In this, she never presumes to know what you *ought* to read.

You slide the paperback copy of Pinter's *Landscape,* which you have read several times, back in its proper place and turn toward Becky's desk. "I have a criticism about the way a certain subject is presented. Who do I see about it? I guess it's the teacher but I don't know that. I don't know how much freedom teachers have to change things. I don't know what alternatives they have or what pressures they are under or what forces influence their planning. It's too simple to lay it all on the teachers, to hold them accountable for everything."

"What subject," she asks moving toward her journal corner, "math or science?"

"How did you know? Why not modern drama?"

"You don't have to know or even study Pinter like you do the Law of Cosines or the Periodic Table. It is neither required nor expected that all tenth grade students understand Albee or Stoppard or Ionesco or Beckett or even

Tennessee Williams. Most English teachers will settle for students just enjoying them. Of the two, math or science, I'll guess math.

Guess you muse. That's a laugh. Becky Feinman is an amazing person. Like all experienced teachers she has developed eyes in the back of her head. She also has flawless intuition, profound predictive powers, and seemingly total general knowledge. It has often been hypothesized that she has a Pentium chip in her second molar on the left and can, therefore, access the internet at any time.

The journal Becky hands you is a quarterly about six months old. It has a simple paper cover which lists five articles. The circulation, you note, is small. It appears to be a joint effort by several local colleges and universities that provide courses for teacher certification. "In here," she says.

"Which one," you ask, scanning the names and credentials of the authors.

"I rather thought you would know better the ones that discuss your questions," she replied, "They're all good."

In her store, Becky has set up a cozy area for reading. There are three rocking chairs, an oak one with a high back from her old front porch and two maple ones. By each is an adjustable floor lamp, also maple. You choose the old oak rocker, turn on the lamp, and start reading the five titles on the cover page. The first one is called *New and Emerging Programs for Secondary Math* by Dr. Stanley Miller. The second is *Making Portfolios Work in the High School Math Class*. Number three is entitled *Curves, Gaskets, Carpets, and Sponges: Working in Fractal Dimensions*. "Whatever," you mutter. Not knowing what portfolios are, much less gaskets and sponges, you leaf through the pages hoping to find a more explicit subtitle or an enlightening first or last sentence. Article four's first sentence...ha! You adjust the lamp and slump into a more comfortable reading position.

Noticing the maneuvers, Becky asks, "Article four?"

You read.

WHO IS BAKING THE PI
By Phillip Dew

Albert Shanker, former president of the AFT wrote, "If we want to change our schools for the better, we have to change what goes on in the classroom between teachers and students." The people in the best position to alter existing conditions in the classroom are, of course, the teachers. Unfortunately, many of the changes that are either being implemented or suggested are driven more by political, economic, or social forces than by sound educational reasons. For the most part, they don't even originate where the teacher is, in the classroom. Consequently, wanting to improve what actually goes on in the classroom often appears secondary to wanting to save money, exercise power, increase profits, or gain personal objectives. Needless to say, changes so motivated are not primarily targeting constructive teacher-student, classroom relationships and may even affect them negatively.

Non-classroom teacher orchestrated steps to improve the teaching of mathematics may be identified as being retroactive, reactive, or proactive. The classic retroactive step comes from the "back to basics" people. For the experienced math teacher, however, it would be difficult to recall any mathematical subject, concept, or procedure that was taught in the 40's or 30's, whatever the acceptable "back to" time frame may be, that is not included in today's curriculum with the possible exception of solid geometry and the use of log tables and the slide rule.

Solid geometry? Oldladydavis would flip!

On the other hand, an exclusive interpretation of "back to" may be suggesting not what we should teach but what we should not teach and when we should not teach it. Perhaps those wanting to back up are recommending that we not teach basic multiplication until the basic third grade or that we not mention such non-basic topics as matrices, field postulates, exponentials or probability during the basic algebra-geometry-algebra sequence.

Which, basically, was algebra-algebra-geometry anyway, you recall.

But then "basics" may be referring to basic methods, not basic content. Rightly or wrongly, it is questionable whether yesterday's methods to motivate and control would be generally effective in schools today. Seating assignments based on grades, a ruler slap on an open palm, or staying after school to wash the blackboard and beat the erasers could play havoc with self-esteem, the law, and the bus schedule to say the least.

One portentous retroactive step was taken when some states and colleges went back to the notion that departments of education providing teacher preparation at the undergraduate level were not worthy of offering a major subject. A weak program at some, or perhaps several colleges, is hardly reason to indict an entire discipline. Rather, it shows an urgent need to strengthen and re-focus the program. Certainly today there is no shortage of excellent research and scholarly debate in the field of education that could improve the presentation as well as the understanding of any of the affirmed major disciplines.

Education, the subject, has too long been viewed exclusively in the narrowest K-12, vocational sense as being simply the mechanics of what people do when they teach. Beyond instruction in routine classroom maintenance and 'x' hours of mathematics, the preparation of a math teacher, for example, also includes those disciplines basic to almost any field of concentration, psychology, philosophy, sociology, and history. Ideally, the field of education should be a comprehensive, integrated, interdisciplinary program of study most worthy of having departmental status and being a "major."

Even so, in Schools of Education and more so where education ceases to be a major, education courses are generally held apart from the subject a student is preparing to teach. The compartmentalization of education and, in the above case mathematics, blurs the focus. If the vital question was "What should math teachers do when they teach math?", what changes in emphasis might be found in the syllabus? Perhaps math teachers would be instructed in the way to teach uses for the quadratic formula, or factoring for answers, or proving the diagonals of a rectangle congruent or, in general, how to teach students to do certain well defined types of math problems. On the other hand, it may be felt that the math teacher should show more what mathematicians do and not exclusively what students do. Maybe in a more expressive, cooperative format, the future math teachers could engage themselves in the process of "making" mathematics. Using exploratory and creative thought processes for specially constructed problems, the student teachers might then experience the same outcomes they would hope to evoke from their students. This would be good too depending on the existing educational objectives. Whatever the combination of courses and objectives, to address the question "What should math teachers do when they teach math?" in a more specific and functional way would sharpen the focus, intent, and effectiveness of teacher preparation.

Education is about experiential exchanges and attitudinal changes stimulated by heroes, needs, concepts, and ideas. The old adage, learn by doing, regarded education and acquisition of skills or knowledge as one. That truism still holds. If that's a "back to" then it is a "back to" worth getting back to. Meaningful opportunities to apprentice and intern yet remain a most effective way to learn.

Actually, locating apprenticeships and internships beyond the formal classroom format is a real possibility if not a requirement in some professions. Finding meaningful variations of the apprentice experience for the classroom is not so easy. Most traditional in-school attempts to learn by doing such as the school bank, investment clubs, a car wash, or a bake sale, have an economic orientation and use little more than basic arithmetic. Beyond the school environs, the "enriching" field trips to art and science museums and places of historical interest are often offered as quasi hands-on experiences. Unless well coordinated by school and museum, such trips may be reduced to entertainment and a momentary interlude. Assuming, however, that apprenticing is an effective way to learn, it should be given a more stable, deliberate place in the curriculum.

Developing new programs, such as "a classroom apprenticeship in mathematics," could be a purpose and an objective of a specially designed student teacher's undergraduate program. Constructive ideas prompted by an augmented and creative education syllabus would lead to beneficial and meaningful experiences both personal and professional.

Having an alternative math syllabus as a viable choice would give schools more flexibility in designing programs balanced in method as well as content. Generally, variations in the methods of teaching math are left up to innovated teachers who want to try something else. Many such efforts are short lived and rarely become integrated in the school math program.

Perhaps because *expressive* ways of teaching math have been repressed by more expeditious *instructional* methods during the 8-12 grades, many young students have developed mixed and confused feelings about what math and school in general means to them. In the extreme. This can be reflected in anti-social behavior ranging from constantly demanding attention to aggressive resistance to total rejection. Such irregular and unacceptable behavior can disrupt, threaten, and even obstruct efforts to establish an ideal learning environment. In such cases, the proper education of many interested and deserving children and the integrity of the system is seen to be "at risk." Thus, of all the long range matters of national security, the best possible education of our next generation should be ranked among the top, particularly if it is as "at risk" as, at times, it appears to be.

Unquestionable, education and culture are the hallmarks of a rich and vibrant society. They are the prime elements that unify and inspire people to do and respect great and kind acts. Education should play a major part in our thinking and planning for the future of this country. And yet, another retroactive step, a step that would abolish the Department of Education, is frequently mentioned in some influential political circles. Comparable flawed and short sighted logic applied to other Departments, agencies, and services at various times in our history could have, by now, reduced government, including the military, the pentagon, our UN offices to loose coalitions of ad hoc committees.

The loyal and patriotic math teachers in the classrooms need to believe that their very real contributions to the future of their country will be , in fact, recognized and that their mission to assist in the education of successive generations of Americans will be supported and represented at the highest level. They and their colleagues need a national commitment embodied in a strong and vocal Secretary of Education, Advisor, or some such Cabinet position, with a proven history of striving to improve the understanding, respect, and dignity due education and educators.

But the word is out. In the newspapers, on TV news programs, in books, from employers, talk shows, and politicians at every election time, the message is education in the United States is in shambles. SAT scores are low, seniors can't read or do math, drugs are rampant, the dropout rate is high, and there are guns in the schools. Why should the public schools and the schools of education and the members of their professional staffs be respected? Their business is a mess!

To these truths, half-truths, misconceptions, exaggerations, and fabrications there follows the inevitable procession of reactive steps. Generally well intended and at times correct, reactive steps, nevertheless, have an unimpressive success rate. Many of these are the "grunt" reactions, longer day, longer year, more courses, more equipment, merit pay raises, and sometimes, more teachers. Whereas the reactive idea may be good, it is the implementation of the idea that often breaks down. Whether it be a lack of understanding, neglect, insufficient preparation, or poor design, one basic cause of failure is not integrating the idea with the entire system, not taking every relevant aspect into account.

The move to establish "state standards" is an example of the all inclusive, multifaceted grunt rationale. To begin, tests have to be constructed and published. In all likelihood, the same publisher will then be commissioned to produce practice tests and review sheets for all the students. This, of course, is an enormous expense not heretofore found in the budget. Not found in the teacher's lesson plans is the time to prepare for and teach to the tests. Not found among the administrator's concerns is the threat that his or her school could lose its accreditation. Never a consideration before, parents now fear the consequences of their children attending and graduating from an uncertified school. Establishing state standards is a challenge grunt that affects the entire system with not the least of its challenges being to justify the disparity of the scores between poor inner city schools with schools in a wealthy, high-tax, suburban, professional community.

Having set state standards, interpretation and enforcement of them is yet another generator of reactive steps. Achieving the standard scores does not necessarily mean improving the educational program. There is very little opportunity for teachers to be creative and for students to explore and express their own thoughts when "practice tests" dominate the agenda. Therefore, where standards are not met, or perhaps where standards are met but the resultant program is too instructional with less time afforded to music, art, and in-depth discussions of ideas, or where, no matter what, SAT scores continue to be low, the drop-out rate high, and acts of violence persist, cries will be heard to remove the Superintendent, get a new Principal, fire the teacher, cut back the funds, revamp the Schools of Education, and demand accountability.

No one, of course, can be held accountable for counter events and attitudes beyond his control. Into this category fall the counter values and consequent behaviors resulting from poverty and deprivation, over indulgence and obsession with material things, hopelessness, parental irresponsibility, commercial exploitation of youth for profit, media producers' mania for large audiences rather than responsible messages, and budget balancers who still subtract apples from oranges. By their diversity and remoteness from the actual classroom, these forces, practically speaking, are isolated and immune from effective accountability. All such unclaimed accountability is ultimately reduced to blame pointing fingers leveled squarely at the education establishment. Sadly, these attacks have been met with silence or attention diverting hype.

In this regard, blind sided math teachers often take a direct hit. SAT exams, for example, consist of a verbal part and a math part. Blame for low verbal scores can be distributed fairly among English, history, and even science teachers. A poor showing in math, on the other hand, cannot be diffused. Not that it is necessarily the math teachers' fault but proximity to the cookie jar is the issue regardless of whether cookies are being put in or taken out.

Comparisons are often grounds for reactive thinking if not actually causing reactive steps. From time to time, Americans are painfully reminded that high school academic achievement at home does not compare favorably with comparable levels in Netherlands, Sweden, Denmark, Scotland, Switzerland, Norway, France and China. Assuming this to be true, studies show that it is not necessarily because of longer days, longer years, better textbooks, better teachers or any other grunt mechanism. We are told that it is because education is highly valued and culturally favored in these countries. Teachers are held in greater respect by the societies.

Surely all American teachers would like to have their profession held in greater respect. Just having their work, their skill better understood by the public would be a helpful first step. Whereas running school systems is a business teaching is not. There is no assurance of quality control either over the raw materials received or the finished product. As a matter of fact, the product is never considered finished and can never be marketed by the teacher. There is no financial profit line and there are no fundamental business philosophies to suggest whether the teaching reflects supply side or demand side principles; i.e. for math teachers, teach pure classical math for any generation or applied vocational math for today. The only aspect of the operation the teacher can control is his or her personal commitment including professional development outside the classroom and preparation for creative teacher-student dialogue in the classroom.

(You put the journal down for a minute. "Becky, were you respected...as a teacher I mean? Did it, or would it have made a difference?"

"Becky Feinman, the teacher, was valued but I'm not sure about the respect part. Looking back, I don't think it would have made any difference to the quality of my teaching though. I just did my thing. You know, I always regarded my teaching style more as an art form. I don't know that anybody else saw it that way. That might have scored a few respect points for the home team," she said.

You think about that one for a few minutes then read on.)

Effective math teaching is more the expression of a given talent and/or the perfection of a learned skill. It is not simply knowing the subject well. Nor is just knowing how to motivate, hold interest, and entertain. It is certainly not "dumbing down" mathematical concepts for the back row. For a start, effective math teaching is knowing what to teach and when to teach it. Depending on the answers to these considerations, it is then knowing the best way to present it. Sometimes this is not easy to do but it is what the competent math teacher must do.

Most retroactive and reactive steps to improve education take place outside the school and effect the teacher and the classroom only indirectly if at all. The sophisticated math teacher, however, would do well to be aware of all the proactive steps that have been taken by textbook publishers, writers of special programs who hawk their own learning materials, and the highly competitive electronics industry that pumps out intriguing software and evermore advanced calculators now capable of graphing all the elementary functions. Much of all this is good, even excellent if the math teacher can keep it all in perspective.

Assume, for example, the existence of a new interdisciplinary math series for high schools called The Whole World Math Program (WWMP). The units of measure go beyond dollars, feet, pounds, meters, and grams. For money they include the franc, lira, peso, daalder, krone, peca, ruble, ducat, and yet among others. Length could be measured in duim, bema, canna, djo, verst, toise, etc. and weight in unze, hao, lood, gros, loth, libra, pood, whatever. The rationale is global understanding.

Though basically a two year algebra course capable of bridging geometry, there are, in addition, numerous allusions in word problems to such topics as the effect of subsidies and regulatory policies on achieving a competitive advantage, tariff and non-tariff barriers as obstructions to trade, floating exchange rates, and the impact of international capital flows. Accommodating this, international units of measure are all interchanged.

Word problems, therefore, may seem pretty weird. Petromarks are compared to petrodollars on the spot oil markets. Kids row up the Po at x canna per hour and down the Maas at y duim per hour. Including profits to France and England, x francs are invested at r% and y pounds are invested at s%. How many rubles should the Russians put out to buy the product at t% assuming a tariff of h%? Determine the average fuel consumption in meters per liter of the five most expensive cars sold in Japan. Stuff like that.

The Whole World Math Program comes with a special atlas, wall maps, posters, charts to fill out, graphs, transparencies, software, and a unique calculator called a "conversion utility," plus a 954 page, 7.3 pound, 8.5x11x1.4 inch textbook with accompanying work books, quizzes and exams with answers, and a teacher's manual, all essential for the proper administration of the program.

The school system bought the whole package at an initial cost to $575 per student plus a matching amount from a local business consortium. They told the public, the taxpayers, that it will change the schools for the better and then they told the non-consulted math teachers that they better produce some tangible evidence that it was working.

Taken as a whole, this is an example of a proactive step toward improving the image of the system with the hope that it may also have some positive effects on what goes on in the classroom between the teacher and the students. It is a bold step taken by its creators, its publishers, its marketing people, and by the politically conscious school system that adopted the program. Clearly this is a gross exaggeration of what could happen. As an extreme, however, it brings into focus some of the far reaching consequences such an intrusion could have on the classroom teacher in particular and the math program in general.

Regardless of the merits of this proactive step, however, there are certain peripheral aspects that bear the careful consideration of the wary math teacher. Immediately she or he will note that WWMP did not originate in the classroom therefore teacher acceptance and preparation could be a factor. Further, the program representing a large commercial investment could be hyped out of proportion by economic, non-educational forces. Also, the program may have been installed for public relation value as much as reform potential. The judicious Head of the Math Department, having the final responsibility for launching

WWMP, must assess its full impact on the existing math curriculum and on the morale and creative spirit of the math teachers, determine options, and carefully chart the best course to follow.

For one thing, needing sales hype, novel programs such as WWMP tend to be illusionary. Compared with its competition, noted the discerning math teacher, the WWMP text has by far the most pictures and cartoons, few of which will ever excite repeat viewing by the students. The colored glossies depict healthy people from all around the earth, happily working in interesting jobs, playing games together, eating a variety of exotic dishes, and moving about freely. The illusion of global well being may be ideal but it just doesn't jibe with the faces. And it has no significance mathematically, added the theoretically inclined math teacher.

The "windows" layout is meant to give the impression that the text is both user friendly and on the cutting-edge of solving two step linear equations and factoring the difference of two squares, for example. Presumably leading the way toward a global math concept, frequency polygons, histograms, quartiles, and cumulative frequency are introduced in chapter three and used thereafter. Aside from the illusion of being on the web in cyberspace, observed the inventive math teacher, the order and depth of the mathematics presented jerks the students around without giving them time to organize and test their own reasonable conjectures. Contrary to the presumed intent of the authors, mathematically, the text is too instructional, too rigid. The students aren't part of the agenda.

Reflecting the recommendations of current educational psychology and learning theory, the authors have dutifully inserted after every third chapter a token "cooperative learning" problem, each conceptually similar to any other problem in the book. It seems hardly worth moving desks around, rearranging the room just to confer about a problem that invites little joint discussion. Professionally, to the pedagogically informed math teacher, the illusion of cooperative learning is demeaning, insulting, and so transparent as to put the whole program at risk. This is one of those personal feelings that the prudent math teacher would prefer to store.

On the other hand, the illusion given by the imposing size of the text, that it is the CD-ROM of algebra 2 books, cannot be ignored. Plainly the Health, Guidance, and P.E. Departments need to be advised that this one item weighs 7.3 pounds and occupies .07575 of a cubic foot. Five such items , a normal course load, would translate into 36.5 pounds and .37876 cubic feet per tenth grader and, with notebooks, a calculator, and athletic socks, an estimated 37 pounds and .4 of a cubic foot. The socially conscious and aritmetically precise math teacher is impelled to inquire, are we prepared to deal with the physical consequences?

With its numerous references to trade deficits, multinational transfers, hyper-inflation, interest rates, and subsidies, the proactive WWMP seems to nurture the allusion that great economic insight is being bestowed on sharp young minds. Perhaps these elaborate applications of monetary systems are only intended to answer the inevitable question, "When will we ever use this stuff?" If so the implied response, "When you become an international banker," doesn't sell either. Thus, exercising their sharp young minds, the students soon learn to cut

through the verbiage and simply "plug in" the given values
for a,b,c,d, whatever in the given formula x = abcd
whatever and solve the equation. The sympathetic,
supply-side math teacher is quietly heartened. "Get to the
math," he says. "I'll take it from there. Soon they will be
using $y = ne^{kt}$ with or without a mitosis or radioactive
decay incentive."

Proactive steps, along with being illusionary and allu-
sive can also be, at times, delusory. Deluding himself
about being knowledgeable with regard to conic sections,
a kid can tap out a parabola on his personal graphing utility, translate it to an auxiliary xy-system, rotate it, and
then bring that sucker home with a single tap on some 2nd
inverse cancel key without any conception of eccentricity,
focal point, or directrix.

The endangered pre-algebra teacher, long since given
up on converting halves, thirds, fourths, fifths, sixths, and
eighths to their decimal equivalence, horrified to see a student resort to a calculator not just for seven times eight
but for three times ten as well. "I got it right," he said.
"Delusions of grandeur," she muttered. Yet fearful of
being out of step, she includes a unit on Operating With
the Calculator after, hopefully, good habits have been
formed. Privately she calls the unit "deferred learning."

The imperiled math teacher stares vacantly at the dark-
ened new 17 "Monitor with its ADM 800 MHz Processor
containing a 30GB Hard Drive and a 32MB Video Card
augmented with an intimidating Multimedia 20X Max
CD-Rom Tower with which he must interface in the fall.
It comes with Bank Works™ , Exchange Change, Safe
Harbor (tracking commercial routes), Float Cash/Cash
Flow, and other WWMP software. It has encyclopedic

information about geography and global economy. Its Class Management program makes assignments, prints out quizzes, tests, and final exams. In a millisecond, each of these may be marked with up-dates of the accumulative average made immediately accessible at site as well as in the administrative office.

Transfixed, the computer generation math teacher who speaks DOS as a second language casually scrolls the Aopen PS/2 Mouse over its pad as he eagerly studies specs, examines port capabilities, checks resolution options, scans files and contemplates in his realm infinite possibilities.

Conversely, having tried dozens of permutations of lovingly refined lesson plans including proofs and derivations of formulas and time consuming graphs, the senior math teacher concedes nothing fits into the WWMP schedule. Even after discarding his always successful project where students discover the quadratic formula in the parabola nothing seemed to work as designed. Process has been sacrificed for answer. It has been said, he recalls, that computers are solutions in search of problems. Where there are only answers, process is lost. Suppose, he wonders, there were problems with no apparent solutions, only process. The ingrained math teacher strains to accept the allusion that WWMP will in some way contribute to the mathematics education of his students as well as conform to the precepts of his experienced professional convictions. Starring back at the silent monitor he asks, "Process accelerator or process eliminator?"

The newly appointed Department Head, midway in her career, has carefully studied the WWMP materials and has heard her department colleagues speak. In a special meeting, all members present and contributing, a plan was agreed upon.

In this rather bizarre model of a well formulated, perhaps over structured program intended to improve mathematics education, it should be noted how far reaching some plans can be, how they may be perceived by those whose responsibility it is to teach the prescribed curriculum, and how they may impact on the culture of the classroom. No matter where they may originate, steps proposed to improve or reform education must be carefully and thoughtfully studied. It must be made clear where the basic ideas are coming from and where are they going. As an abbreviated outline for such a study, it is suggested that the critical elements of the plan be identified and evaluated as to how they reflect both constructive and inappropriate retroactive, reactive, and proactive thinking.

Wow! You wonder what those math teachers would have to do to pull the WWMP thing off. Inwardly you feel they could and would...but how?

You hand the journal back to Becky and just stand there thinking of the right thing to say.

Holding up a thick blue journal she removes the need to say anything. "There is a good article in here by Howard Gardner," she says.

Finally, not wanting to get into it now, you simply thank her for her help adding that the

next time you might get her to order Jacques
Barzun's book about western cultural life.

"I have two copies," she says.

RECESS

A dillar, a dollar,
A ten o'clock scholar,
What makes you come so soon?
You used to come at ten o'clock
But now you come at noon.

PART 5

▼

ENNIS RYAN

You remember Johnny telling you about the teacher he had last year in geometry. His name is Mr. Ryan and according to Johnny he is "weird." On the other hand, all the students including your son like him, said he is smart, fair, and a good teacher. But he does dumb things like start at the end of the chapter and work back or sometimes skip the whole chapter saying no Greek in his right mind would do it that way. He doesn't follow the precise order of topics as presented in the textbook which leads some parents to complain that the course isn't "structured." He never uses the tests provided with the text. Every test he gives is original and tailored just for a particular class which leads some parents to complain that without textbook facts and procedures to memorize there is no way to study for his tests. Instead of just doing the $a^2 + b^2 = c^2$ thing , he proves the Pythagorean Theorem several ways including something called Perigals dissection. He teaches some ancient history and science and gives examples of plane geometry theorems worked out by familiar names such as Ptolemy and Pascal which leads some parents to complain that whatever it is Mr. Ryan rambles on about it isn't on the SAT and certainly won't help their child's GPA. Mr. Ryan doesn't care what they think which leads some parents to complain to the Principal, Mr. Gage, who listens intently while secretly marveling at the brilliance of his off-beat teacher.

Mr. Ryan, of course, isn't crazy or weird or that off-beat. He just has strong principles and a few counter annoyances that get him fired up. For one, he violently resents the geometry textbook and the "contrived" way it presents the subject. To the Greeks, he would remind the class, geometry approaches being a philosophy, a religion not to be reinvented. And as such it remains to him. Mr. Ryan also hates a disordered forum and therefore loses patience with some of his colleagues during faculty meetings. He knows more about parliamentary procedure and Robert's Rules of Order than any of them and doesn't hesitate to call "point of order" when the English teachers stray from the discussion topic. He is also capable of moving the opposite of what he and most others want just to get some trivial technicality that a history teacher is pushing voted down and out of the way. In addition, his running irritation with the school board and the city council often gets aired in the "Letters" section in the local paper to no lasting avail.

Ennis Michael Ryan is his full name. It is said that he all but took his vows to become a Jesuit priest but then got married instead. At six foot six he would have made a pretty imposing priest. His voice is deep and has great resonance. When he stands, he seems slightly bent forward, as if looking down on his flock. His dark hair is evenly trimmed on the side but stands up in wild curls on top. He wears dark rimmed glasses when he reads in class which isn't often. A very mobile face enhanced by a pair of expressive and totally independent eyebrows equips him to be uncannily effective at non-verbal communication. His basic look of distaste bordering on anger is juxtaposed against a quick and wry humor that can disarm and dissolve a class into riotous laughter and even applause, apparently, as he sees fit. "Actually, Mr. Ryan is cool.".

It does not surprise you, therefore, when at PARENTS NIGHT Bob Willard hands you the latest epistle from Ennis Ryan. "Your de-stuffing problem?" Bob queried., "he's on your side. Read this."

You skim the first paragraph then ask, "Did anybody publish it?"

"The NCTM returned it. That's all."

"What now?"

"It's yours," he said.

     *   *   *

This is an open letter to all those people (p) who will decide what the math curriculum (c) will be next year (y)

or the one after (y+1) or any of the years (y+n) such that
(y+1) is between (y) and (y+n).

Dear (p);

While some people are reinventing things these days,
why not you reinvent (c)? It needs it again. If what there is
put us where we are, there is no way we'll get the gold by
2000 at the International Trimathalon, if it really is a goal
and, if it still is, that should be reinvented too.

Admittedly, to change (c) all at once would be unthink-
able, unwise, and unnecessary. It is also "non-probable"
the way things get reformed in education. Fortunately, the
sequence of courses from pre-algebra to calculus is conceptually consistent and workable with the exception of the
intrusive digression into the mathematics of ancient
Greece. A course in Euclidean geometry inserted between
two algebra courses benefits the essentially algebraic
sequence about as much as Latin , stuck between French 1
and French 2, would enhance proficiency in French.
Whatever so called plane geometry is meant to contribute
to (c), it should definitely do it someplace else.

Ever since the post Sputnik "new math" reforms of the
late 50's, (p) saw fit to relieve geometry of its once held,
exalted, upper stratum status as the purveyor of logic,
pure math, and reasoned truths. Not only that but with
the removal of solid geometry, it was even stripped of the
practical consideration of being a prerequisite to some
logical successor.

Yet, perhaps out of misguided respect, it was deter-
mined that geometry could remain in the high school
sequence provided that it dress up its act with the appearance of "sets" and whatever traces of the theories of Galois,
Abel, and Boole that could be worked in. One wonders

how much more Thales, Pythagorous, Euclid, Appollonius, Archimedes, and their many contemporaries would have contributed to geometry had they conceived of an angle as the intersection of two subsets of lines AB and AC such that AB is the set of points AB and all the points Q for which B is between A and Q and AC is the set of points AC and all the points R for which C is between A and R, B and C not being collinear.

Thus, with mind clogging pomp, the "new math" writers of the 50's and 60's superimposed on Greek logic the mathematical logic of the 19th Century. Bandying about lofty images of "congruent adjacent angles with non-common sides forming opposite rays and the intersection of line AB with the set of points A, B, and C such that AC +CB = AB, they strained to demonstrate their skill and fascination with misplaced rigor. While confounding with renewed abstraction, the writers of geometry textbooks succeeded by the end of chapter two in both obscuring the beauty and historical significance of Euclidean geometry and forever losing student interest and momentum.

Yet , toward the middle of the text rigor is diminished, there are fewer proofs, and the problems have become more numerical. By the final chapters, the writers have abandoned once and for all, not only the two column "steps and reasons" proof of Grecian logic but also their insistence on using the logic of the 19th Century. They basically condone the practice of allowing students to memorize and apply formulas for angular/arc measurements, areas, and volumes. From the students' perspective, the degree of difficulty seems to have been mysteriously inverted, as if it matters by that time. Therefore, without clearly establishing a necessity for geometry or even its historical significance in the process of mathematical evolution, the once proud subject now comes off to many as being one of those boring, useless, inexplicable irritations that must be endured to satisfy graduation requirements. You might say it's enough to create an identity crisis.

Geometry as a full year course needs to be rescued and placed out of the algebraic sequence. For its survival, it needs to be alone yet with meaningful reminders discreetly placed throughout the sequence. Since the sequence ends with calculus, which is necessarily preceded by pre-calculus, the prerequisites of which are algebra 2/trig and algebra 1, the only place for plane, Euclidean geometry is before algebra 1. Both pedagogically and historically this, in fact, is the proper place.

The course that now precedes first year algebra, so called pre-algebra, is notoriously a hodgepodge of mathematical one liners. Whatever it contributes to algebra 1, or anything else in the sequence, is all repeated in contexts more meaningfully and appropriately introduced later on. Instead, pre-algebra could be "early math," an historical introduction to the methods and intrigue and development of mathematical thought, perhaps up to the Renaissance where modern math begins. Why not? The mathematics included would be topics from the amazing algebra of the Egyptians and the Babylonians, the syllogistic logic of Grecian geometry, the evolution of many of the signs and symbols that students use today, and some of the early achievements that lead up to the great works of Descartes and Newton.

There are sound reasons for supporting the math taught with its history. No one doubts the need for and importance of history to thinking, rational beings. It provides them with points of reference, a sense of continuity, and defines their "place." Every system of education in the world includes courses in history. And yet, students can go through years of living with mathematics not suspecting a vibrant history exists, a history that would strongly contribute to their personal understanding and appreciation of mathematics. Pre-algebra geometry is a good place to introduce and use history to show the attraction and power of mathematics and the thinking that produces it. Needless to say, this historical approach to mathematics should continue throughout the algebraic sequence.

At the 8th grade level, geometry can do for the algebraic sequence what Cuisenaire Rods does for the arithmetic sequence. Using areas and pattern analysis, distribution, factoring, the Pythagorean Theorem, and many other concepts important to algebra can easily be "seen." In both algebra courses, geometry can be used to create novel and timely word problems. For example, the following could be used after studying a unit in sequences and series:

PROBLEM
In triangle ABC, an altitude CD is drawn to side c. From the foot of the altitude, a perpendicular is drawn to side b and from its point of intersection on side b, another perpendicular is drawn to side c. In this manner, perpendiculars are continuously drawn between b and c. Examine the altitudes or perpendicular distances for possible relationships. Make conjectures about your findings. Develop proofs for the conjectures.

A possible conclusion to this problem is the following:

THEOREM

Corollary: In right triangle ABC, right angle at C ; $h_n = a\left(b^2/c^2\right)^{n-1}$. The length of the altitude to side c (CD or h_1) and all the other perpendicular distance to c are members of the geometric sequence $<h_1, h_2, h_3,....,h_n>$. Where CD = h_1, DA=m, and CA=B, it can be proven that $h_n = h_1\left(m^2/b^2\right)^{n-1}$.

It might further be noted that geometry has the interesting non-mathematical capability of modeling abstract ideas. At some basic visual level, having a sense of cones, warps, and holes, we can read about the existence of time cones, warped space time, and black holes with less confusion than seeing the pages of symbols, formulas, and equations that precisely define them. On a day-to-day level, we all have a "circle" of friends until being "triangled" by two of them. And the image of eating a "square" meal while pleasant and clearly understood, bears no relationship to that quadrilateral that is both equilateral and right angled. In the math classroom, being able to model conics, velocity, derivatives, and integrals, et. al. on a Cartesian plane is absolutely essential. Showing geometry as an important model building branch of mathematics should also be part of the pre-algebra geometry course.

In my opinion, a geometry course of this nature would not only tighten up but also lighten up the high school math program. A properly designed pre-algebra geometry course would create a year for more math or for other non-math interests. It could also be a new and vital point of contact between students and teachers. Most importantly, it would rejuvenate geometry giving it, once again, a purposeful place among all the algebras and making them better for it.

Cordially,

(r)

*   *   *

Tim Gage is talking about a new roof over the cafeteria and the possibility of getting lighting for all the tennis courts so that more people can play at night. Some parents are talking about the band not practicing outdoors so late in the evening and why couldn't they do it in the gym. Bob Willard is reminding parents about PROGRESS REPORTS coming out next week and encouraging parents to make appointments with teachers should they have questions or suggestions. A mother gets up and offers a particular Thank You to the driver of bus number seven for finding her daughter's term paper. Mr. Ryan is sitting tall in his usual place on the outside aisle, half way back. He knows you are reading his letter.

RECESS

As I was going to St. Ives,
I met a man with seven wives:
Every wife had seven sacks,
Every sack had seven cats,
Every cat had seven kits.
Kits, cats, sacks, and wives,
How many were going to St. Ives?

PART 6

▼

STANLEY J. MILLER, B.A., M.A., PH.D.

Although you still have no definite idea how to make Johnny's math course more real to him so that he will see both purpose in it and areas of personal interest, you do believe that the de-stuffing problem is opening up. Mr. Brill did describe for you a profession as old as civilization itself that grew out of human need as well as genuine intrigue. Clearly it is the result of a continuous, worldwide interaction of the most brilliant minds of every age. Remarkably, it maintains inviolable integrity as it attempts to solve the ever-present array of contemporary problems. Surely such a disciplined profession would welcome appreciative and productive student interest and may even contain clues as to how this may be attained.

Bob Willard, being a math teacher himself, made it clear that to become a math teacher and teach math is a very special experience because of math's unique set of symbols and cool abstractions not intuitively known or embedded in the culture or the every day life of the family. Because of these unique aspects of math teaching, you suspect, the job of de-stuffing math, in the last analysis, must fall to the teacher. He's the guy in the classroom. Besides his training and the crazy symbols and the material he has to teach, what else does the math teacher carry with him into that classroom that might help? As Bob Willard would express it, "what are the invariants and what are the variables"? In most school situations, the textbook is not a variable. It has been bought and paid for with taxpayers' money and must be used. If the teacher wishes, he can change the order of the topics to be presented but must cover in the end all the material listed in the syllabus as prescribed by the State Department of Education, Division of Mathematics or whatever group up there that makes such decisions.

In his letter, Ennis Ryan writes of not merely moving topics around but moving a whole course out of its sequence perhaps requiring a different text. Actually, his idea does make sense to you except that part about the theorem and its corollary. Even so, you concede, geometry taught with an historical spin before algebra could help in the objective of de-stuffing math. It would certainly tie in with Tom Brill's plan to develop some sort of a math time-line. Usually, assuming there is enough time, the teacher is allowed to add subject matter or enrich the course if desired. The time-line idea within a classroom is feasible but moving geometry to a lower grade could be rough no matter what the merits may be. So, if the invariants are the syllabus, the materials, and the schedule, what are the variables? The methods of instruction teachers chose seems to be largely up to them. This could be a key variable to the act of de-stuffing math. What, you wonder, are the going options in pedagogy?

A hand written note brought home by Johnny informs you that there will be, as part of the city's Faculty Development Program, a lecture at the school next Thursday at 7:30 PM. The last sentence says, "Look forward to seeing you again," and it is signed Bob.

You arrive at the school auditorium about 7:15. There are only three people there and they are sitting together. You move over to their general area and sit about six rows behind them., three in from the left aisle. The three teachers, sitting up straight and looking forward at the drawn curtain, turn occasionally and whisper to each other. You hope somebody else will come as you start looking around for Mr. Willard. At 7:23, groups of people, walking quickly, begin to enter. The procession continues, intensifying in both numbers and noise. By 7:30 about 60 people are seated. Bob Willard enters from a door near stage left carrying a light, portable lectern and places it in the center about even with row one which is empty. A woman wearing a mustard colored beret comes in by the same door. She has an extension chord and a light that clips onto the lectern. Mr. Willard finds the outlet for the chord and the woman tests the light. It goes on then she turns it off. It is 7:38 and the only thing not apparent is the speaker.

Bob Willard goes to the lectern, turns the light on and says, "Welcome to the third lecture in our Faculty Development Program. Teachers, you are reminded that if you need points for purposes of re-certification, you may use this Note of Attendance to verify that you were here. If you want one of these, raise your hand and Miss Teague will pass them out now." The lady with the beret moves quickly to the center aisle, counts the hands up, gives the right number of Notes to each person sitting in an aisle seat who then passes them across. That done, Bob Willard looks up at the audience and says, "It gives me great pleasure to welcome back to our lecture program Dr. Stanley Miller whose talk tonight is about a matter that I am sure will be of great interest to us all, Education Reform. Ladies and gentlemen, Dr. Miller."

The gentleman sitting two seats to your left stands and, walking to the lectern, takes some notes out of his coat pocket. He shakes Mr. Willard's hand then places his notes on the lectern. "Thanks Bob. Thanks again for the opportunity to teach a class where I don't have to read papers or average grades (polite laughter). Should you wish a copy of my remarks tonight, give your name and school to Bob and I will have it sent to your school's office. These notes, by the way, will contain footnotes and bibliographical information for those of you who are writing journals for your graduate courses (groan)." Then, as all speakers do, he opens with, "Can everybody hear me?" Assuming they can, he begins. It is now 7:45.

"The process of reforming education is very complex which is one reason why reform is slow to come about and difficult to notice when it does come about. To bring the process into more clear focus, I am going to zero in on the steps necessary to make one simple addition to one already established program. I have chosen the mathematics program because it has a syllabus which has basically remained constant throughout the entire twentieth century. For all you teachers of other disciplines, I submit the steps and reasons applied in the example of math will hold for your subject as well. Please bear with me."

"Ahem!"

(The following is the printed copy, with references, that Dr. Miller provided.)

It is felt that the luxury of making the restrictions of content and the pressures of time subordinate to centering on process and developing understanding does not come often enough in the high school math curriculum. Nor is the unswerving pursuit of higher and higher math (until the inevitable drop out point) often altered by the warnings and reminders of leading educators and psychologists. They have often advised that students need to feel that their education is an evolving, personal experience over which they have some control being actively responsible not only for how much they learn but also for what they learn. Also, allowing students to exercise expression for creative and imaginative ideas, they believe, is an integral part of the learning process.

For example, needed but not often found in the secondary school math program, is a summary course employing cooperative learning opportunities, portfolio assessments, open ended, adaptive thinking problems along with narrative, future thinking critiques. It is believed that such a course, consequently, would have a high potential for generating a diversity of responses, reflective abstraction, positive interdependence, intuitive thinking, as well as utilize multiple abilities and interpersonal skills. Further noted, "The power of the adaptive view is that it offers an explanation of...how an intellectual process might start from nothing" (Bailey, 1996, p.52). Research has often shown that a learning environment which provides for and purposely encourages greater self-monitored student involvement in areas personally meaningful to them, greatly enhances conceptual understanding of the material.

Yet typically, course choices for the students who have met their minimum math requirements for graduation are pre-calculus for the fast track, finite or discrete math to embellish the transcript if nothing else, or general-whatever math for whatever; again, content oriented, predictive instructional courses. The other possibility, too often the sad option of choice, is to drop math altogether.

It seems that there is both a need and a window of great opportunity after the completion of the algebra-geometry-algebra sequence to offer a student oriented course which deliberately targets process and understanding. Not being a priority, new content need not be introduced but could and would arise naturally out of the positive interaction of the cooperative groups and the students' need to understand and explore each others ideas.

For the record, the new course must be given a name. In the custom of naming courses pre-this or pre-that, i.e. Pre-calculus, logically the course could be called "Post-algebra" but the regressive connotation would be both misleading and hard to sell. However, since it is not so much a course as a program that provides opportunities for students to wrap things up for themselves before moving on or getting out, let's say program, not course, and call it WRAP-UP math.

It is recognized that popular thinking tends to regard a program so structured as being remedial and not appropriate for the "good" and "best" students. For those very able students, eager to begin careers in mathematics and science, WRAP-UP may not seem to be their next best step. On the other hand, it could be a most challenging experience, particularly for creative, motivated students. For the majority who intend to drop math or possibly hang on through a semester of calculus in college, WRAP-UP could be their only self-directed, creative, and personally meaningful experience in mathematics. Further, seeing the process above the algorithms might even encourage some students to linger longer in the domain of mathematics.

Allowing, for example, that WRAP-UP math is the one change we want to implement, let us follow the steps that could lead to its ultimate acceptance in the math program. The first thing any step to reform should do is assert a need and establish a sound professional rationale for a change in or inclusion to the existing high school program.

There seems to be no doubt that the need for a more expressive, student oriented course exists but to what extent? College counselors and math teachers may even agree that WRAP-UP is a great idea, yet conclude that there simply isn't enough time to offer it. The need, it would be said, isn't sufficiently strong to cause the possible postponement of calculus much less its disappearance from the high school transcript. As a response to this argument, in an unpublished pamphlet for perspective students on selecting their high school courses, the Core Standing Committee (1993) at Harvard University recommended the following:

> To acquire the mathematics background you need at Harvard, you should study mathematics every year in secondary school. But simply taking mathematics is not enough. You should acquire the habit of puzzling over mathematical relationships....It is the habit of questioning that will lead you to understand mathematics rather than merely to remember it, and it is this understanding that your college will require....The ability to wrestle with difficult problems is far more important than the knowledge of many formulae or relationships.... do not rush into calculus....In the last analysis...it is not what courses you have taken but how much you have thought about mathematics that counts.(pp.6-7)

To show the professional rationale for the inclusion of WRAP-UP math, let me review for you some of the current writings of prominent educators addressing problems related to designing new learning programs. That problem, in its most simple form, becomes finding the optimal match between student and material (Gardner, 1985). More broadly, Goodlad (1984) suggests "the most successful classrooms may be those in which teachers succeed in creating commonly shared goals and individuals cooperate in ensuring each person's success in achieving them" (p.108).

Traditionally, at the high school level, the math curricula is driven by a standard body of content and a requirement that the material be covered in a set period of time. For the most part, the teaching is instructional, the lessons learned uniform, and the results predetermined. Serious inquiries into student interests and "play time" with graphs, shapes, and patterns are incidental if they occur at all. Only in so far as these activities augment the basic lesson plan and time permits would they likely become an integral part of the course.

On the other hand, in lower schools, Eisner has noted "Elementary school teachers...are often sensitive to the changing interests of the children they teach, and they frequently attempt to capitalize on these interests, 'milking them' as it were for what is educationally valuable" (Eisner, p.32). Also focusing on the learning environment, Kantrowitz and Wingert (1989) express the importance of hands-on, physical activity in the classroom. Studies show, they point out, that the most effective way to teach young kids is to capitalize on their natural inclination to learn through play.

In high school math classes, play is still effective though it may better be described as an imaginative examination of mathematical concepts or a creative composition of logical events or, possibly, an expressive search for the unexpected. Through this sort of play, it is possible to identify a student's interests and stage of development. "As much as possible," Gardner says, "we must bring the teaching to where the child is" (Siegel and Shaughnessy, 1994, p.564). Similarly, as noted by Brandt (1990), David Perkins places great import on the interconnectedness of the "culture" of the classroom, subject matter, and general thinking skills.

Supporting these general objectives but with greater specificity, Clark (1986) has found that "students strengthen their inner sense of control by learning things they value and that meet their needs" (p.64). She also urges the use of strategies that encourage future thinking, imagery, stretching the mind, intuitive awareness, divergent thinking, and production. Intelligence is dynamic, Clark believes, and schools must develop an environment that can respond to each child. Referring to needs and environment, Glasser (1992) concurs adding that learning situations should offer need satisfying projects in an atmosphere free of coercion and they should have opportunities for self-evaluation.

Clearly the needs induced by a cooperatively explored mathematics project would originate from the group. Being novel and open ended, the project would invite imaginative solution strategies requiring the formulation and testing of conjectures. It would also prompt sufficient conceptual understanding to recognize and question patterns in the data. At the conclusion of the project, each member would have the chance to propose and discuss any additional ideas that the results may imply.

The practice of students working together cooperatively toward a shared goal, with group members succeeding or failing as a unit is called cooperative learning (Johnson,D. and Johnson, R., 1987). Armstrong (1994) points out that cooperative learning is but one of many current alternative educational models that are essentially multiple-intelligence systems using different terminology. As an MI system, he notes, "cooperative learning, for example, seems to place its greatest emphasis upon interpersonal intelligence, yet specific activities can involve students in each of the other intelligence's as well" (p.49).

A cooperative learning group should have joint learning goals, a project with complex assignments requiring multiple talents and abilities, and be non-hierarchical. Further, the group activity should be carefully structured to include a high level of positive interdependence or face-to-face interaction. The members should be held individually accountable for their share of the work. They should think about how well they work together and what they could do to improve the quality of their work. It is, therefore, important that they be taught the interpersonal and small group skills they need to coordinate their efforts (Johnson, et al., 1993).

Kagan (1989) and Ellis (1990) are in agreement with the Johnsons, particularly in the areas of interdependence and accountability. Kagan adds that acceptable structures for a cooperative group would not include such activities as painting murals. In his words, it should have a "content-bound" objective. Referring to the teacher's responsibilities, Ellis includes monitoring student's behavior, giving feedback, intervening when necessary, and offering roles to play, individual tasks, rewards, and a group product. Because of the multidimensional format of WRAP-UP in which the teacher has a shared part, an additional teacher responsibility would be acting as a combination mentor and master craftsman to apprentices, available for observation.

There are several interesting models of cooperative learning which have been experimentally and practicably applied to the classroom. Kutnick (1990) cites three including one based on research undertaken by himself (Kutnick and Brees, 1982):

> The focus of his investigation was on the development of relationships in a close social sense. The study structured sensitivity exercises to promote trust and dependence in classrooms of 5 year-old children. When compared to control and individualized groups, the experimental children developed similarly in an academic sense, but were more socially sensitive and aware of other children's perspectives. (p.92)

Skills of social perception-taking or decentering are, Kutnick claims, are at the base of the transition from pre-operations to concrete operations.

The second cognitively applied, collaborative approach described by Kutnick has focused specifically on the transition between pre-operation and concrete operations. The cognitive conflict generated between peers engaged in solving a problem is seen as the basic mechanism promoting transition:

> Cognitive conflict forces peers to decenter, acknowledge and allow for other perspectives in their own thinking. Cognitive conflict is generated...only when there is a mutual (non-hierarchical), participatory, and non-individualized "learning situation"; that is, equal peers must work together to solve a problem—not just observe one another or told what to do. (p.93)

For this approach, Kutnick cites the work of Perret-Cermont (1980) and Bearison, Magzamen and Filardo (1986).

The third model of cooperation is taken from the work of Slavin (1983). Kutnick points out that Slavin centers on two distinct components of an instructional system: the task structure in the presentation of the curriculum and the incentive structure. A wide range of documented improvements have been attributed to Slavin's research and programs of cooperative learning:

In comparison to control groups (who were given similar, but non-cooperative learning experiences), cooperative learning pupils showed consistent academic improvement, overcame barriers to "within school" friendships (crossing racial and sex discriminative lines), and were able to work effectively in mixed ability groups (sometimes incorporating handicapped children). (p.92) In addition to these models of cooperative learning, many more have been designed and researched. Further, cooperative learning strategies such as The Six Thinking Hats, PMI (plus, minus, interesting points), and APC (all points considered), have been contributed by deBono (1970) and others.

Among the many methods of Student Team Learning (STL) in use, Slavin (1991) lists six, which he considers to be the main ones. These are STAD (Student Teams Achievement Divisions), TGT (Teams, Games, Tournaments), TAI (Team Assisted Individualization), CIRC (Cooperative, Integrated Reading and Composition), JIGSAW (learning from the text is stressed), and Learning Together (group investigation). In all, the central concepts are team rewards, individual accountability, equal opportunities for success, and positive interdependence or shared group goals.

Taking exception to Slavin's emphasis on rewards, Kohn (1991) believes that extrinsic rewards encourage ego over task involvement and that they tend to weaken creativity. Slavin (1991) nevertheless defends his position saying extrinsic rewards can and do expand the content field and motivation. He recognizes other controversies particularly regarding higher order skills noting, however, that whereas benefits of cooperative learning have been well documented for grades 2-9, there has not been sufficient research on its effects at the 10-12 grade levels to make claims either way. In general, he feels that there is a strong consensus of agreement on the major principles of cooperative learning.

Students working cooperatively, on a group activity, with a common goal, individually accountable for a share of the work, present a situation radically different from the traditional classroom structure. A resultant pedagogical problem is "how to transform what has traditionally been regarded as a linear process of knowledge acquisition into a multifaceted system" (Leinhardt, 1992, p.21). Such a system, she insists, must include both the content of the field and the actions or activities of the field. Related to this is the problem of helping students focus on the "deeply principled aspects of knowledge as opposed to the shallow ones" (p.21). Principles, performance, and conceptual understanding, therefore, should be seen as arising out of the act of working together.

Gardner (1991) has also expressed concern that students today are being taught surface-level knowledge without ever affecting their deeper understanding of the world. Students well stocked with mathematical postulates, algorithms, and principles still resort to previously learned misconceptions, rigidly applied procedures, stereotypes, and simplifications. "What is required is an approach to education that challenges naive beliefs, provokes questions, invites multiple perspectives, and ultimately stretches a student's mind to the point where it can apply existing knowledge to new and novel situations" (Armstrong, 1994, p.152).

Eisner (1985) advances the idea that to achieve greater understanding, educational methods should focus on process and not outcomes, and that they should be expressive rather than instructional. In the traditional, predictive instructional system, an indication of achievement is unambiguously defined by the terminal behavior and homogeneity of response is desired. Expressive methods encourage diversity of responses. When meanings become personalized, children produce products. As in artistic criticism, the object is not to dictate outcomes but to appraise techniques:

> The expressive objective is intended to serve as a theme around which skills and understandings learned earlier can be brought to bear, but through which those skills and understandings can be expanded, elaborated, and made idiosyncratic. (p.55)

An expressive objective, Eisner says, "provides both the teacher and the student with an invitation to explore, defer, or focus on issues that are of peculiar interest or import to the inquirer" (p.54).

Further justifications for greater accent on expressive educational objectives are voiced by Elkind (1986). Arguing that there is too much emphasis on right or wrong and quick predetermined responses, he notes that most formal educational techniques such as flash cards, rote memorization, standardized tests, and the stress on algorithms provides little opportunity for reflective abstraction. Self-directed learning, he suggests, promotes reflective abstraction from those activities and positively affects self-esteem, motivation, and curiosity.

The self-directed concept of Elkind does not seem to differ in effect from Slavin's individual accountability in cooperative learning. Nor is it unlike Gardner's (1993) position that learning is enhanced when children are allowed to self-monitor their own work and be actively responsible for what and how much they learn. Elkind believes that children acquire knowledge best when it is related to their own sets of abilities and interests.

Consistent with the advantages of a cooperative group working toward a shared goal, Gardner also holds that "intelligence skills are effectively implemented when used in service of a particular goal" (p.129). In pursuit of this goal, he believes that children benefit from a focus on process as well as product. Broadening this theory beyond academic content, Gardner contends that "practical intelligence skills are most powerfully integrated when presented in both scholastic and real-world contexts" (p.129).

Sternberg (1988), taking exception to Gardner's theory of multiple intelligences, believes that intelligences may not be independent and that they may be more akin to talents than skills. He does, nevertheless, rely heavily on experience and the external world along with the internal world of a child to complete his triarchic theory of human intelligence. Intelligence, he believes, must contribute to the child's ability to adapt. Perhaps not multiple intelligence but, according to Sternberg, there are multiple aspects of intelligent self-management to help cope with novelty in the external world.

This research that I have briefly sketched out for you has included the culture of the classroom, cooperative methods of instruction, instructional and expressive educational objectives, theories of intelligence, and an expanded view of the curriculum which relates meaningfully to the external, real, outside world. The final element of investigation is to examine alternative assessments appropriate for evaluating a group, multifaceted project.

In assessing the work of a cooperative group, Perrone (1991) would de-emphasize grades and encourage risk taking. He recommends the use of critiques, practice tests, student appraisals, and portfolios. He would incorporate in the culture of the group or class that the primary concern be the success of the whole class and not a select few, individual "number ones." Whatever combination of assessments are used, they must be wholly consistent with and arise out of the activities of the program.

Of particular relevance to the ideas of Gardner, Krechevsky (1991) feels that assessments should be set in real world activities using those adult standards that fit the child's stage of development. Rather than focusing on the skills in a school context, she prefers assessments which directly pertain to the abilities needed to achieve successful adult roles. For this, she examines multiple areas of cognitive ability. Gardner (1991) concurs calling for "assessments in terms of meaningful adult end states that are valued by the community" (p.244).

Expanding on the idea of adult end states, Heath (1994) believes that such can neither be accurately predicted nor defined in terms of a one or two dimensional aptitude. The adult end states or characteristics of maturity deemed most worthy reflect a broad understanding of intelligence with a full range of abilities. He speaks of being a self educating person as an ideal state inferring the need to develop divergent or adaptive thinking skills.

Similarly, Sizer (1992) values the ability of students to employ knowledge in new situations. Using "Exhibitions," he directly targets comprehensive educational outcomes by having students demonstrate mastery over a broad field of interests.

It was noted earlier that to accomplish any revision in a standing program, the initial task is to assert need and establish sound professional rationale for the proposed change. In the example of recommending that a WRAP-UP program be added to the high school math curriculum, the proponents would probably take additional caution not to criticize the traditional courses either for content or methods used in teaching them. WRAP-UP would augment the math program. They should, nevertheless, make clear their findings that the need, the pedagogical justification, and the time needed to offer WRAP-UP definitely exists.

And on that note, let me end this session with a question. "How many here will be rushing to your Department Head or Principal tomorrow about making changes." (All hands go up. Bob Willard puts his hands over his face.) "You've been an excellent class. Thank you very much."

(Applause).

"And thank you Stan for that welcomed suggestion," Bob adds, walking to the lectern. "Teachers, all proposals should be typed, single spaced, with documentation. no less than 100 pages and sent to Dr. Miller for additional recommendations." (Mixed applause and booing followed by laughter). "Seriously though Stan, I am sure we have all gained from your remarks and I certainly do thank you for coming here tonight. I for one, regard the curriculum as an evolving program and that possible revisions should be on everyone's mind. Changes do not come about easily, probably because the system is so large, not because the ideas are too bizarre. So, take heart teachers. Keep those new ideas coming. Local changes can sometimes be made and, perhaps, if presented as Dr. Miller suggests, they may benefit your school and even the district if not the whole system."

Dr. Miller returns to the lectern and invites a few questions from the audience. The lady in the mustard color beret stands and says, "Yes, I have a question. We are talking mainly about changing things from the bottom up. As you know, they can also be changed from the top down and in a hurry too like the changes in math and science after Sputnik. My question is this. If national standards come about. could that bring about another sudden change in the curriculum?"

"Liz, that is a very good question. It, of course, begs another question. Can the federal government impose national standards on the individual states? If it can, that will be a major change it itself. However, to address the intent of your question, let's assume that a state has either accepted suggested national standards or has establishes new standards of its own. I would say that it is unlikely that standards will target traditional content, the so called "basics," in a course. After all, the thrust of new standards is simply to get higher scores across the board. These may be used and interpreted in a number of different ways. For international comparisons, it can be shown that students in our system are learning more facts and achieving greater skills than students in some other systems. For business and industry and professions, we can say we are bringing forth young people who are better prepared to define and solve problems."

Dr. Miller pauses and backs away from the lectern for a moment. "With an emphasis on scores however, likely changes are apt to occur in the methods used. There could be less time for experimentation and innovation. Those teaching methods that work will be stressed. For example, if outlining history gets higher scores than reading it and if drill works best for math facts and if Cliff's Notes on Portrait of an Artist (which is not on the test) allows for more time spent on Hamlet (which is) , and if the scores determine whether a teacher will get a raise, a bonus, a remedial class, or be transferred to another school, you can guess which methods will be used. Any comments on that?"

"I'm bothered," said a man sitting directly behind you. Dr. Miller, seeking the source of the voice looks straight at you You lean far to the right, exposing the man, making possible direct line of sight transmission which you hope will be forthcoming. Slowly standing the man says, "I don't teach math but I don't suppose it matters. Didn't I hear you say that educational methods should stress process not outcome?"

"Yes! That was Elliot Eisner's feeling and I agree with him. What is your concern, sir?"

"Dr. Miller, the longer I teach English, the more convinced I am that there are multiple intelligences. I agree with Howard Gardner totally. Do you think there can ever be standards for real linguistic intelligence or bodily-kinesthetic intelligence or intrapersonal intelligence? Do you think the processes used in developing linguistic intelligence, for example, can ever be fairly assessed? Frankly, I don't and I wonder, what meaning will the scores have for students strong in these areas? I mean, for these intelligences, how can process be assessed?"

"Very good questions," Dr. Miller says smiling at the group. "Let's have one more and then we'll try to come up with some answers."

"Dr. Miller," a voice says from somewhere on the other side of the auditorium. "All these expressive teaching techniques, portfolios, cooperative learning and all that, it seems to me that a great variety of outcomes will be produced. How in the world can you make standards for all of them?"

"Let me first say that I hear your questions," says Dr. Miller, "and they have been mine too. I hear as well the principles beneath your questions and suspect they are strong and forged out of your experiences. Here is my solution. I will allow that national testing of certain basics has a place in our vast school system. It may help some students, some teachers, and some schools. It is up to the educators to keep the outcomes in perspective and not let politicians or the media put a skewed slant on the scores to further local interests or some political power play. The testing may take one or two hours in a given year. The rest of the time is mine to explore MI Theory, to set up cooperative learning groups, to use portfolios in assessing student work, and to continue with my program of professional development."

There is an immediate and approving response from the group. Not wanting to cut short the applause or extend the meeting beyond the approaching hour, you nevertheless stand up. Being near the front, everyone sees you and abruptly quiets down. Typically, the questions asked have all gone off in one direction. The mustard beret mentioned standards and that did it. You know it is too late now but you haven't been able to work Dr. Miller's need and rationale idea into your de-stuffing problem. You wish the mustard beret lady had asked something about making changes from the bottom up, from within the school. You recall the journal article Becky Feinman gave you. To bring about a change, it said, you have to change what goes on in the classroom between teachers and students. You want to hear about that kind of change. Suddenly, sensing the nature of the silence around you, as if it were a "get-on-with-it" sort of silence more than a respectful "your-turn" silence, you say something stupid and unnecessary about not being a teacher but finding his lecture most interesting and provocative.

That did it. The teachers get up. Some walk out. Many go down to say something to Dr. Miller. The lady in the beret is among them but she is probably waiting to unclip the light and take it back stage. Bob Willard approaches and sits in the seat next to you. "Chicken," he says. You admit it then thank him for inviting you to come. "I know what you were going to ask," he says. "But we'll get into it.

I'll arrange a time when you and I and Tim Gage can have an uninterrupted hour or two, how about that."

"Who's the beret?" you ask.

"Liz? That's Elizabeth Teague our librarian," Bob says getting up. He joins the dwindling little group around the lectern.

Using the side aisle, you quietly exit.

RECESS

Kick up tables, kick up chairs
Throw our homework down the stairs.
No more pencils, no more books,
No more teacher's ugly looks,
No more things that bring us sorrow
"Cos we won't be here tomorrow.

PART 7

▼

TIM GAGE

Hardly your typical public school principal, Mr. Gage never taught in a public school, didn't even go to a public school, only recently became certified as a secondary administrator, and has absolutely no interest in moving up to the Central Office or, for that matter, moving out of his present office for any other position in the system. But that has sort of been the story of his life.

Tim Gage grew up in Bristol, Connecticut where he attended a small private day school. When he reached the ninth grade he was sent to one of those independent boarding schools that sit on top of every other hill in the north western part of the state. At Wyncrest, he continued to be your basic "good" student, not excelling but still taking some of the advanced courses offered. The biggest change that came over young Tim was an immediate eagerness to be involved in every phase of school life. The athletic policy at such schools was that everybody had to be on a team regardless of grades and there was enough variety and lower levels of teams so every student could learn to play and participate in some sport. His first year, the "third form" year, he played third football and basketball and went out for crew. They rowed fours at Wyncrest, not eights. His senior write-up in the yearbook reported that he was the Prefect for his hall, Co-editor of the school paper, Honor Council, Varsity Football (two years), Varsity Basketball (one year), Varsity Crew (three years), Captain of Crew in his sixth form year, and Head of a group called HELP. This was a student organization that he had started to serve the community in many ways like helping to harvest crops, put out serious brush fires, control the often flooding river, and provide peer tutors in the town schools. Tim loved Wyncrest and made many lasting friends including Mr. Colbert, the Headmaster.

Upon graduating, he went to Princeton. The University's many opportunities to pursue different subjects and fields of interest seemed inexhaustible to Tim. He wanted to check them all out. Entering his senior year, he had amassed a broad, seemingly random medley of courses but with no declared major. Reviewing Tim's transcript, an advisor expressed amazement that there had been no formal effort to satisfy any departmental requirements. He did note with obvious relief that Tim had inadvertently acquired two and possibly three "default" options. If he took an extra heavy load in either psychology or history or possibly mathematics, he could fulfill the "concentration requirement." Tim majored in psychology.

Along with no strong feelings about a major at Princeton, Tim had no idea what he wanted to do, or was able to do, after Princeton. He, therefore, welcomed Mr. Colbert's invitation to return to his prep school on the hill where he could teach and coach while pondering career choices. He would teach math, coach third football, and assist his old coach with crew. Nine blissful years later he became Assistant Headmaster working mainly with fund raising and development. After three years, Mr. Colbert retired. Actually, the Board of Trustees had decided that it was time for the all boys school to switch and become coed. Mr. Colbert quite rightly felt that the school could make this change a lot easier than he personally could and suggested that Tim Gage be the one to "guide Wyncrest through its exciting period of transition and on to fulfilling its new mission."

Once again Tim found it prudent to accept Plan B. As psychology was his default major at Princeton, so had education become his default career. Being in charge of a school, however, forced Tim to be more in charge of himself. From then on, he would not be living out his back-up options. If he was going to be head of a school then he was going to be head of a school that he would believe in.

Feeling strongly that his school wasn't deliberately nurturing all the skills or intelligences that students have, he made what would have been an impossible change in the former all boys school. Tim modeled an arts policy after the athletic policy that had meant so much to him. He built a strong fine arts department that offered music, drama, dance, and visual arts with the requirement that every third former would experience each of these during the year. After that, students would be expected to be engaged in at least one artistic course or event each of their remaining school years.

Perhaps his most controversial plan came in the area of assessing student progress. Historically, the school had always used the 100 point scale with 60 being the lowest passing grade, no grades to be issued in the 55—59 range, and any grade below 40 on the final to result in failure for the year, no exceptions. It was believed that such rigidity preserved high standards. Beneath this iron-clad inflexibility, however, there were numerous human variables that made the system quite acceptable. Some teachers, for example, were harder than others. Some gave frequent quizzes while others gave few. The home-work that was collected was either checked or chucked. Extra credit problems, lab reports, term papers, projects were all used and evaluated in different ways often depending on the "needs" of the class or a particular student. Further, in many cases, teachers made up their own final exams and therefore were accountable only to themselves. The system, while unyielding at the surface, did provide for "professional compassion" within.

Imprecise as this system could have been, it worked. As Tim said to his faculty "While I am asking you for a critical evaluation of our system of assessing students' progress, with recommendations for possible changes, I must confess that for me, at the time I was a student here, everybody knew the system and somehow we all made it work. The teachers were all dedicated professionals and at no time, to my knowledge, were the standards compromised. I am not at all sure, however, with the sophistication and quantity of material we have to teach today, and the changes in work ethics, that students and teachers can any longer make it work. The climate has changed and perhaps we should too. I don't believe we should rely on a tacit understanding between students and teachers to make it work. Furthermore, on a more general note not directed at Wyncrest, I must add my belief that today, reports should show what students know, what they can do best. I do not trust standardized, objective tests to tell me all I need to know about our students. Knowing how well they can cram or get correct answers without understanding the processes is not relevant. Least of all, do I want to dwell on what students don't know. What they do know and where they are intellectually is what is important. That is precisely where teachers should meet them."

Tim proposed classes that used cooperative learning techniques throughout the entire year. He also asked the faculty to consider alternative methods of assessment, particularly using student portfolios. He set up faculty committees to research all the possibilities and also to consider the feasibility of such changes being accepted and working in the school.

The faculty worked hard on this project. They read journals and articles and books on the subject. They visited other schools where students prepared portfolios or produced some major project or "exhibition." They met and discussed and passed around frequent status reports. After six months, in May, Tim called a meeting of the faculty for a final discussion and vote. In a split decision, the faculty voted to keep the grading system as it was citing tradition, standards, and preferences of alumni and parents as the determining factors.

Actually, Tim expected this and was fully prepared to accept the decision and keep the old system working. During the next seven years the school grew, achieving a healthy balance of boys and girls. Remembering the vote on alternative assessments, Tim privately admitted to his wife Kim that he still had a lingering regret that he missed the chance to experience the fun of such an open system. She said he would find fun in doing old things in new ways or just plain doing new things in some other place.

Kim's words passed as a typical summary remark until the next spring when they attended Tim's 22nd Princeton reunion. There, his roommate Marty Stockton, famous for impersonating Jimmy Stewart, asked in that familiar voice had Tim ever thought of "doing public?" He had an opening coming up in his district and could have "his people" set it up if Tim was interested.

After ten years as Headmaster of Wyncrest, Tim considered the advantages of a change both for the school and for himself. The cycle of leadership had gone full term and, good as it was, he couldn't see going through it again. Of course, Marty as a member of the school board couldn't really pull off a switch to the public school as he had jokingly implied. He did strongly recommend Tim to the Superintendent who, after a thorough search, did offer Tim the position. Tim arranged to stay at Wyncrest one more year, giving the school time to find the right person to "guide Wyncrest into its ever promising future." Subsequently, an aspiring young lady from Virginia accepted the call and became the first Headmistress of the

once proud boys school on the hill. And Tim, living out
the fruits of Plan B, ended up in a Principal's office.

This background on Mr. Gage came from Bob Willard.
Your son has told you that Mr. Gage is all over the school.
He is in the halls, comes into classes, even eats in the cafeteria. He watches teams practice, sits in on play rehearsals,
and occasionally takes his trumpet to band rehearsals. It is
generally believed that he knows everyone in school by his
or her first name.

You ask Bob about this. "Does Mr. Gage get too
involved with the students? Does he play favorites? Are the
teachers jealous or amused by this? Does it interfere with
his administrative duties? Basically, does the school trust
and respect Mr. Gage all the way?"

"Absolutely," Bob says, "no question about that. Its like
he is the teacher and the whole school is his
class…only…he doesn't teach. I mean, he isn't telling
people what to do all the time. He isn't instructing. He
supports and shows interest like he wants to know what it
is we do best and then see that we get a chance to do it.
For sure, if our best isn't good enough for the job, he tells
us that too. No, if Tim has any problems with respect, it
is more likely to come from one or two other Principals
who don't understand his ideas about leadership.

Today, Mr. Gage is having one of his small meetings, or
preceptorials as he calls them, with the Math Department.
As you and Bob enter the library you see Tom Brill, Ennis
Ryan, and four others all ready seated around a table. Mr.
Gage gives a sweeping wave biding you to have a seat. Bob
briefly introduces you to the group. There is Nancy and
Ken to your left, Arne and Lois to your right, and between
them two empty chairs reserved for you and Bob.

Tim holds a thin, black, spiral bound, vinyl covered
register in his hand. "The subject is grades. Calibrating the
concerns and methods of mathematics with the names and
numbers in this grade book has me wondering. What is it
that these grades are grading? Grades are data generated by
teachers and students, not the concepts taught. With them
and in terms of them only, it can be proven that a student
honored, passed, or failed. But, it is said, what is provable
is not necessarily what is true. Right, Tom? You're the his-
torian here. What is Mr. Godel telling us?"

Tom gives me a quick look then leaning forward
offers, "Might Kurt Godel be saying in his
Incompleteness Theorem no system of grading can ever
produce all true statements about the achievement of
understanding concepts?"

There are smiles all around and even some soft clap-
ping. Tim, among them says, "I knew I could count on
you." as if this were something that happens often..

"Or even stronger," Tom continues, buoyed by this support, "for every consistent formalization of averaging
grades, there exist arithmetic truths that are not provable
within the formal system?"

"Exactly," Lois adds, "yet, those grades were given with
such assurance and finality based on the evidence. But if
not truths, then what were they grading?"

Funny question for a department head to be asking,
you think. What if some parent whose kid didn't make the
honor roll or failed heard that? You look at Ennis Ryan to
see what you can learn from his expression for surely if
something were amiss, he would show it.

Ennis is not sitting tall which you take to be a good
sign. Furthermore , he seems to be anticipating with relish

the opportunity to take some startling stand. Bob said that this was a preceptorial and not a faculty meeting. You decide to sit back and see if you can't figure out what Tim's preceptorials are.

Tim speaks. "Assessing student performance is one of the aspects of teaching where the teacher's preferences and personal priorities are most pronounced. The same syllabus, text, supplemental material, length of term, and final exam can produce very dissimilar grades. Though more apparent in subjective courses like history and English, differences in assigning math grades occur as well. These differences, for better or worse, primarily affect the students and can shade their feelings about the subject. The seemingly theoretical question, 'What do grades grade?' has a very real application to the learning environment, or as David Perkins might say, the culture of the classroom."

"For example, assume a school system with a minimum passing grade of 70.0. For simplicity, let's say there are four, nine week grading periods and the final grade is the average of the four." Tim hands each a sheet of paper on which grades are listed. "In the class, five students failing to make the minimum, received the grades you see." On your sheet is written:

Student A: 0   70   73   76   Average 69.8
Student B: 50 70   75   82   Average 69.3
Student C:40   70   80   86   Average 69.0
Student D:86   80   70   40   Average 69.0
Student E: 40 70   80   76   Average 66.5

"Now," Tim says, "in particular, what can we say about these final, failing grades? What do they grade?"

Ennis pounces on this one. "If they grade achievement, fall achievement shouldn't be weighted the same as spring achievement? You have to reward progress. If the grades grade progress, how about having a standard "grade differential?" A student starting with a 76 and ending with a 76 would have a "gd" of 0, indicating no progress. Should he pass? Student C had a gd of +46. That could do it for him." Ennis thinks for a moment then asks, "All right, which one of you is going to mention the poor slob who started out with a 20 and brought it up to a 66. I concede to Kurt Godel on that one. The gd system of grading cannot produce all true statements about passing grades."

Arne says, "Your gd idea may not be a consistent mutually inclusive system but it might be a subset of the system, just like effort. There is no scale on which to grade effort but we all know that your gd is a function of effort."

You are keenly aware that you are in the presence of math teachers. Who else would be into subsets, inclusive systems, functions, and inventions like a gd this early in the meeting?

Ken, who is usually the first to turn in his grades, comments, and anything else that is due, says "On the other hand, doing grades can be treated as an automatic, one-step conclusion as well as some complicated weighting of variables. It can be whatever you choose to make it."

Picking up the handout Tim says, "For each hypothetical student on this sheet, you all, well all but Tom, can probably think of a dozen real cases. For example, Nancy, without giving the real name, who is Student A?"

"Student A is definitely Carl. A classic over-achiever. Not too swift in math. Works his head off. Also plays soccer in the fall. Gives it his best 110% of the time (that's coach math). 76 is the highest grade he has ever made."

"Does Carl deserve to pass his math course? Can he handle algebra 2/trig next year?" Tim asks.

Lois says laughing, " There is your +16 gd, Ennis, plus a heavier weighted spring grade should take care of the low soccer season grade."

"Steady improvement. I like that," says Ken.

"I know what I did," says Nancy. "I passed him, only it was a her and she played field hockey.

Ken says he'll take Student B. "Picture me as a slightly younger guy originally hired to coach lacrosse but slipped in to teach geometry when a need arose. Let's see. Student B is Rita. Her older brother was a math whiz. My best student. Was awarded the Tech Math Prize at graduation last year. Cool guy too. Yeh, Rita could use some of his smarts. Just barely passed algebra 1. What did I say her grades were this year? Hey! Not bad for her."

"Is that it?" asks Tom.

"As I have said before," Ennis asserts, "opening a geometry text is like opening a can of worms; all terms and principles and postulates and definitions for things most students either know quite well or never heard of. In math, you learn by doing and here there is precious little to do. No wonder Rita's first grade is so low. Typical!"

"So in this case, the grade reflects the material used, in particular the text," says Lois, "and the effect is carried right up to the final mark which it dominates."

Arne, who tends always to be the student's advocate says, "I'm not sure how I would explain it if the issue came up but I would modify the first grade with what I saw happening in the last marking period and Rita would clearly pass."

"No argument there," Ken says smiling, "but I'd like to see your math on figuring her final grade."

"I gave her a 76," Arne says. "Go figure.

"You didn't count the 50," Tom says immediately.

"What 50?" Arne says and there is general laughter as everyone readjusts to his or her chair.

You are thinking how math teachers love talking in terms of numbers. You wonder how short this meeting would be if they used letter grades instead of numbers.

Lois reads, "40, 70, 80, 86 averaging out to a 69.0...that's a laugh. Maybe not exactly those grades but remember, a couple of years ago, that girl who moved here from New York City? Had been to some inner city high school. She made an A in algebra there but her course apparently did not include much on rational expressions and nothing about quadratics or inequalities. We let her try algebra 2/trig since the first part is pretty much review of algebra 1. She learned fast, improved all year and in the end wrote a super exam. Got the identities right...the focus for the ellipse...the sequence problem...well done Unlike Student C, she passed. As a matter of fact, that girl went on to honor and was awarded a full scholarship at Johns Hopkins. Any questions?"

Student D reminds Arne of a girl named Ashley. She was smart but lazy. Her usual pattern was to start out with high grades on the easy stuff then float through on minimum effort and crease the course with a 74 or so. Student D blew it. "How about Ashley?" Nancy asks.

"You know me," Arne says. "I agonize over cases like Ashley's. You remember how friendly she was, popular, full of fun, always in a group laughing, always doing anything but school work. She blew it too."

"I had a string of numbers like that in my class last year," Nancy volunteers. "Call him Michael. He was a senior. Unlike Ashley, Michael tested poorly in math and suffered math anxiety as well. He was repeating algebra 2 and some of the early stuff was still with him. He was doing all right but after the mid-years he started to slide and when we got to trig, he was totally lost. He came for extra help as often as he could. Somewhere in all that, it occurred to me that he would never need or see a sine function again. In any event, he needed the course to graduate. I reworked his exam and found points I could give him for his algebraic manipulations. In the end, his average was 71. Move over, Arne, I'm a softy too."

"Student E is like a kid I tutored," Tom says. "He was having a lot of trouble at the beginning and when his first grades came out, his parents asked me to work with him. All was going well, steady improvement, good attitude, all that until the spring. A few weeks before the exam, his teacher told him he would have to make 100% on the final to pass. The poor kid had never made 100% on a test much less on an exam. He more or less threw in the towel, gave up. 'Why bother,' he said. He took the exam and even though he hadn't studied for it, he did get 75 or something on it. Anyway, it wasn't the perfect paper he needed. He failed."

All the teachers around the table are silent. It occurs to you that they are wondering about the quality and professionalism of math teachers everywhere and how by comparison they stack up. Your efforts to de-stuff math have brought to light several of their concerns. Are they

teaching the right material? Should it be compartmentalized in the existing order? By what methods do they teach
math and how skilled are they in using these methods?
How kindly and yet realistically do they assess the
achievement of their students? It seems to be for each a
quality moment of introspection.

Sensing a return to unity in the group, Tim looks
around the table and says, "We all know there are those
teachers distinguished for dismissing every issue with the
comment, 'that's not my problem.' They might say,
'Socioexcusonomics aside, the kids failed. It is clearly
stated in the Handbook To Students that a passing grade
starts at 70%. 70 is THE number and they didn't come up
to it. Ergo, try again next year guys. Q.E.D.' Yet you, on
the other hand, are telling me that since there is no
absolute value for, say 80%, our grades, even with projects
and portfolios, are at best a guide. Then, where is the rest
of the grade? What would make it more nearly absolute?"

Lois laughs. "Think of trying to figure out what was
in the remaining 20%. Exactly, what 20% of what I
taught didn't he get? If you can answer that, then try to
determine exactly the 80% I did teach. Add the two up
and you get 100%.

"Would that include your lessons on honesty and
responsibility and how to fold quiz papers," Nancy quips.

"Back to your question, Tim," says Ennis, "if you are
looking for the rest of the grade, Marshal McLuhan would
say its with the grader, his 'the grader is the grade' thing.
Thus the teacher-grader can count the hardest problem
the most and put it first. That alone can cut the average
student's grade in half. Or he can slip in an irrational ratio
in the geometric series problem and watch even those who

got it right the first time spend ten valuable minutes in disbelief trying to fix it before settling on some wrong rational ratio. Average in zeros for homework not done with earned quiz averages (Eight quizzes with an average of 86 plus two missing homeworks, for whatever reasons, equals 68.8). Award zeros and twenties, grades from which recovery is hopelessly doomed. Do all or some of that and you can put the 70% wherever you want."

"Conversely," says Nancy, "a measured array of "warm fuzzies" such as colorfully decorated special projects, cut and glued models of pyramids, optional, one question quizzes on rote memorized material, and encyclopedic reports on famous mathematicians, could raise any grade to an agreeable level."

"Then there is the old 'fudge factor,' says Ken, "plus or minus x points that can be applied in close situations. Ultimately, of course, one can apply an indecipherable yet mathematically consistent 'scale,' capable of generating, translating, and skewing bell curves using even the insufficient sampling and statistically insignificant data of a grade book. With such an instrument, everyone can pass. However, if The Office insists, all but the statistically anticipated lower 13% can pass with the upper 13% reserved for honor grades. Yes, it is in the realm of possibilities, therefore, that math teachers can raise, lower, pass, or fail as they jolly well see fit…heaven forbid"

"Then in any school," Tim says, " there can be found teachers ranging from the tough but fair and impartial autocrat all the way to the benevolent, understanding, patient, 'resourceful' grader. However, not to judge, each extreme can be effective and there are students who do thrive best under either one system or the other. Wouldn't it be safe to say that most math teachers are in between and have the flexibility and the skills to slide in either direction as befits the situation?"

Ennis suggests quietly, "of equal importance, the teacher should ask if his method of assessment is appropriate to the way he teaches? A clear distinction exists between instructional and expressive methods of teaching. Similarly, some teachers stress arithmetic competency and strict adherence to prescribed form. I use a more conceptual approach emphasizing process. Others believe students should master the algorithms of the text before experimenting with different methods. Admittedly, I jump around in the text capitalizing on student interest and conceptual readiness. Some jump in and out of the text voicing their own interests and/or topics of expertise."

"I follow the text," Ken says, "but I really don't regard the given chapter sequence as sacred much less pedagogically proper. I can work with it."

Tom is dying to say something. "Whereas teachers reward unusual originality and imagination only when it appears, I openly and deliberately try to arouse creativity in my students. I like to put them in novel situations like keep the rules but change the setting. Let the y-axis be a parabola instead of a straight line. That sort of thing. I try to put them at starting points and see where they will go. Is that OK?"

"I beg your pardon," says Lois feigning disapproval. "You do what?"

The others are displaying mock horror. Ennis's thick eyebrows are raised almost to his hairline. Then there is laughter and genuine expressed interest in Tom's idea.

"Math teachers should be aware of differences in teaching styles," Tim says, "and the resultant secondary objectives. The fact is, they can organize and present their lessons in a variety of ways. For the most part, this is a healthy sign. It is the teacher being expressive."

Lois reminds the group that regardless of the effectiveness of the method and skill of the teacher, however, at the end there is an examination of some kind. "What a student expects of the test and consequently prepares for is a function of what and how that student was taught," she says. "To teach one way and test another would have to be regarded as being either deliberately tricky or thoughtlessly irresponsible."

Bob continues this line of thinking saying, "Along with presenting mathematics, building and collecting reliable data on which to judge student achievement is a collateral teaching skill. Mathematics may appear to be a very impersonal, emotionally, lethargic subject congruous with a dispassionate assessment process. However, nothing can point out to a student his shortcomings as quickly and irrevocably as a miserably low grade on a math test. Opinions and interpretations, worth a try in history or English, are useless ploys in math. Therefore, though the subject may seem to be impersonal, the overriding effect is to the contrary. Knowing how to prepare a class for a test, how to construct an appropriate test, and how to evaluate the results of a test are among a math teacher's most valuable skills.

Although it is not immediately apparent to you, everyone else senses that the preceptorial is over and that the objectives have been met. Rather than discovering something it is more like new commitments were individually found and pledged. The thought occurs to you that you have just experienced cooperative group learning. You aren't sure why but you do have a better understanding and appreciation of Tim Gage. He makes being naive a virtue, successfully improvising a talent, and staying focused a gift, perhaps even one of Gardner's intelligences. His goals are simple. His mission is to find truths in a profession that indeed may be a default profession to him but to which he owes no dues and from which he carries no scars.

Bob walks close to you as you leave as if you may need support. What seemed light and airy at the time now seems profoundly fundamental. "See what I mean," he says.

RECESS

See—Saw, Margery Daw,
Jack shall have a new master.
He shall have but a penny a day,
Because he can't work any faster.
Jack shall have a new master,
He shall have but a penny a day

PART 8

▼

LIZ TEAGUE

Bob told Tim and Tim told Liz that you were doing some sort of research on the teaching of mathematics, at least that's the way it came down to Liz. The de-stuffing part never made it. Just as well, you think. You haven't figured it out yet anyway. As a matter of fact, you are clueless, as Johnny would say.

You are standing outside of Oxbow Books seeing what Becky has put on display. Over the window curtain, you notice a lady in a green beret. It is, of course, Liz who is talking to Becky about having a book exhibit at the regional math conference which is coming up. She seems glad to see you and says she has been meaning to speak to you about doing something for the conference. You assure her that you would be happy to help out and thank her for asking you. "What would you like," you say, "helping with registration, handing out programs, setting up meeting rooms?"

Becky looks at you knowingly. "I suspect it is something of a different nature," she says.

Liz then explains that, after talking to Tim, she thought it would be interesting if the teachers heard from a parent in addition to deans, educational psychologist, and other teachers.

"A very provocative idea," you say, "but what would the parent talk about? And teachers might not want to hear from a parent anyway. They probably get enough of that."

"You could ask them if they know why they became math teachers. Did they choose to be math teachers or did they just fall into it? Would another subject have been better? How do they feel about thinking analytically all the time, dealing with abstractions and strange symbols? What is it they are trying to teach?" Liz looks at Becky and says, " You know, I could never teach math."

"The library does suit you better," Becky says.

"Hold it!" you say. "Surely you are not suggesting that I give a presentation."

"Don't say no now," Liz says moving toward the door. Gotta' go. Think about it and we can talk later. Thanks Becky, we'll be in touch."

"You knew, didn't you," you ask Becky.

"Green hat," she says, "Liz is into lateral thinking."

"Lateral thinking?"

"Edward deBono. I have two of his books on it."

The next day you see Tom about the possibility of having to prepare a talk. He makes copies of some of his college notes. He also lets you borrow three of his books and strongly recommends two others. After that, you go to see Bob. He tells you that Liz would like you as a parent to say something but you don't have to. Liz is an amazing organizer, he says. She can jump from one issue to another, change directions, and improvise at the last moment. It would be all right if you decide you can't do it. She would simply open up another probability and go from there.

In the next few weeks, you read Tom's books and get another from Oxbow Books. You work up a couple of drafts about the de-stuffing math problem and start a third but the more changes you make, the further you get from a solution or any satisfying conclusion. You decide to try what Liz had suggested about choosing to be math teachers but before you start you check to see what Becky remembers about that conversation. With her help, you outline a few of the central issues and decide to go ahead and see what comes out. When you are finished, you make a couple of copies and leave one on Bob's desk.

There comes a time when math teachers should close their classroom doors and think alone for a moment about their chosen profession; why they chose it, what its all about, and how they are handling it. Being a teacher of mathematics is not like any other teaching assignment.

Particularly, it's not the cut and dry, right or wrong, subject that some people think it is. For a counter argument
to that point of view, consider how Langer (1942)
regarded mathematics and mathematicians.

> Mathematicians deal only with items whose
> sensory qualities are quite irrelevant. Their "data"
> are arbitrary sounds or marks called
> symbols....Behind these symbols lie the boldest,
> purest, coolest abstractions mankind ever
> made....The mathematician does not profess to
> say anything about existence, reality, or efficacy of
> things at all. His concern is the possibility of sym-
> bolizing things, and of symbolizing the relations
> into which they might enter with each other. His
> "entities" are not "data" but concepts. (pp.27-28)

This is hardly the description of a right or wrong situation. Dealing with irrelevant sensory qualities, professing
nothing about the existence of things, communicating
with the purest, coolest abstractions ever is what the "if
and only if a math teacher" may have to accept as his "bottom line" when the fun and games are all over.

Such severe constraints do not apply to other disciplines. In no other high school course are the conclusions
disassociated with reality or in isolation from the natural
world an initial condition. Without external winds and
currents and oceans blue to sail, Christopher math teacher
must proceed from the seemingly trivial reflexive principle, for all numbers n, n equals itself.

Imagine how this physically vacuous origin might affect
the appearance of the properly representative math
classroom. With sensory qualities being irrelevant and

having nothing to profess about reality, the professionally correct math classroom would probably be bare. Perhaps a few vicarious bids to the real world would be allowed. For example, a black and white photograph of Einstein standing in front of a chalk board with abstract symbols scrolled on it or a colorful reproduction of the Mandelbrot fractal would suffice. Then too, like cursive alphabets and numbers running around the second grade classroom walls, the math classroom could legitimately display a generous sampling of arbitrary, symbolized abstractions. A bit stark perhaps but, on the other hand, a completely bare classroom has its advantages. To that inevitable question, "When will I ever need this stuff?" one could always look deliberately around the room then fire back, "What stuff?"

There are other major consequential differences in being a math teacher. Think for a moment about the lessons going on in other classrooms. What are they talking about? What drives them? Quite likely there are some anthropocentric discussions of truth, love, tragedy, conquest, and discovery. Surely, somewhere, students are weighing, heating, dissecting, mixing or, in general, observing fragments of reality and collecting data. Perhaps they are committing to page or canvas impressions of beauty, leisure, tension, or the common place, all recognizable human experiences. Elsewhere, there may be an intense concentration of physical and mental effort, attempts to bring into harmony individual motor skills and specific coordinated, muscular objectives.

In the non-math classrooms down the hall, there seems to be an awareness, acceptance, celebration, even willful conformity to the precept that man is a social animal. Quite apparently, those teachers and their students share, from the start, common, intrinsic bonds. They have a decided head start. Given all this, why would anyone want to be a non-non-math teacher?

Nevertheless, there exists an enthusiastic group who are or will become math teachers for various reasons. Perhaps because of their love of, fascination with, or possibly successes in the study of mathematics, some decide to teach math. That is, because of the mathematics involved, they become math teachers. Others gravitate to it because, foremost, they want to be teachers. Teaching math may be a viable option but teaching, pure and simple, is their profession of choice. In order to teach, these people must declare a subject and some actually declare mathematics. Then there are those who did not intend to become math teachers originally but for whom math is a possible skill that could be developed. They are looking for challenging work or are changing careers or, to pursue a coaching or latent teaching interest, accept math teaching as a means of getting started. It is a good exercise for math teachers to reflect on how they happened to end up in their classrooms and whether or not they are privately glad they did.

Ideally, math teachers should be totally comfortable with and have mastery over the material in their teaching domain. The teaching domain includes the sequence of courses preceding the one being taught as well as the course or courses that immediately follow it. The teaching domain should also be open ended in that there needs to be a knowledgeable appreciation of new developments in technology, current and emerging programs, and the changing alignment and significance given to conventional material.

Whereas formal study of material beyond the teaching domain may contribute immensely to an individual's professional growth, it probably has a limited and delayed impact on the actual lessons in progress. Contrarily, concurrent in-depth study of "domain related concepts" could lead to new and creative teaching techniques as well as providing greater insights and understanding of how the material may be used in the classroom.

Part of any math course should be a conscious, conspicuous effort to make known and firmly establish the true province of mathematics. To this end, it is often said that mathematics is the language of science or, more specifically, the language scientists use. Thus it would seem being the medium through which scientist communicate is what math is about. Indeed, this is so. Physical theories can be formulated mathematically and new concepts can arise from the resultant, derived equations. Reflecting on the vital and unique function of math, Pais (1991) makes the following comment:

> Mathematics plays a many-splendored role in physics, from the coding of experimental results in terms of numbers to the formulation of physical laws in terms of equations. We do not know why the language of mathematics has been so effective in formulating those laws in their most succinct form. Nor can we foretell whether this will forever continue to be true. (p.176)

Historically, there are numerous instances where scientists developed precise and consistent mathematical formulations of theories they believed to be true, often before the full meaning and consequences of the theories were realized. For example, the conceptual implications of the quantum theory, even after the mathematical formulation was complete, proved to be "shattering" to the physicists' mechanistic Cartesian-Newtonian perception of reality. Describing the situation, Capra (1982) writes, "The new physics necessitated profound changes in concepts of space, time, matter, object, and cause and effect; and because these concepts are so fundamental to our way of experiencing the world, their transformation came as a great shock" (p.77).

Without any formal obligations to reality, mathematics has its flip side to the process that produced quantum mechanics. In that case, there was first the theory then the proper math to substantiate it. Regis (1987) recounts a "converse" scenario where Paul Dirac proved abstractly the existence of positive electrons or antimatter one-and-a-half years before they were actually identified in a Cal-Tech cloud chamber. In addition, Hawking (1988) tells of two predictions resulting from the mathematics of Einstein's General Theory of Relativity of 1915 that were not scientifically verified until years later. The first, that light is deflected by gravitational fields, was confirmed in 1919 while the second, predicting time to appear slower near a massive body like the Earth, wasn't verified until 1962.

The language of mathematics has certainly enabled scientists to analyze data systematically and, more importantly, formulate apparent theories and infer others yet to be realized. In his classroom the math teacher, awestruck by the achievements of his profession, may dream of how exciting it must have been to be working cooperatively with Albert Einstein, Niels Bohr, Louis De Broglie, Werner Heisenberg, Erwin Schrodinger, and Wolfgang

Pauli: how enormously thrilling to have contributed to the formulation of the theory of quantum mechanics. Such, he concludes, must be the quintessential pay-off for being a mathematician/physicists.

Still, if not quite quintessential, there must be some lesser yet authentic "x-essential" pay-off that he and his students could experience. To duplicate the quantum experience, it would take a group, a theory, a mathematical formulation, and projections. There must be the potential for unexpected results. As phrased by Casti (1990), "unsolved problems are the lifeblood of any intellectual activity" (p.359). Inventive results, developments, discoveries often occur when people are trying to adapt to new ways of looking at things. Perhaps traditional structures and systems would have to be changed to set up fresh, novel conditions requiring the need to think adaptively.

In any event, to say that math is the language of science is surely correct and very necessary. By itself, however, it is not sufficient to define the full realm of mathematics. Math is as well the language of stock brokers, cooks, engineers, car salesman, and sports statisticians. To some degree, math is a language for everybody. Obviously math includes numbers and having no numbers in our daily routine would produce about the same effect absolute zero has on molecules. Using math is an everyday activity, hence in schools there is increased emphasis on applications or "word problems." Students are shown that the physical world needs math and that they definitely need to know how to use math in that context.

Mathematics however, as perceived by Langer, really does not need the physical world to justify its existence unless, of course, it is agreed, using that old philosophical argument, that trees do fall silently in the forest where there are no ears to hear them crash. Without heights to measure, interests to compound, budgets to balance, the math necessary to perform these functions would still be there. It might be pushing it to say that calculus was around before Newton happened to notice it. But math is a composition, a logical collage of concepts: terms, postulates, principles, theorems, corollaries, and conjectures. The interrelation of these concepts becomes more vivid as they are arranged and rearranged by mathematicians over the years to fulfill the needs of both function and curiosity.

The concept of limit, for example, enabled the classical geometricians to proceed from the area of a regular n-gon to the area of a circle. Newton used the concept of limit to describe mathematically instantaneous velocity. In both cases, zero had to be reckoned with. The Greeks were faced with polygons whose sides were reduced to points of zero length. Newton was dividing distance by a time period of instant, or zero, duration. While Newton didn't invent the concept of limit, he certainly put a new spin on its meaning. By giving limit a formal Cartesian definition, he was able to creep up on zero, ever close, without having actually to get there.

Perhaps more out of curiosity than functional necessity, mathematicians also played with the notion of self-similarity long before Mandelbrot established explicitly the mathematics of fractals. Peitgen et al. (1992) gives an excellent survey of classical fractals from the Cantor set and the space filling curves of Peano and Hilbert, to the often displayed Koch curve, the gasket and carpet of Sierpinski, the Menger sponge, and the exotic sets of Gaston Julia.

Somewhere between the mathematics generated by need or function and the mathematics generated by curiosity, there exists the domain of "pure mathematics." The field is rich with the ideas, failures, and successes of mathematicians. Casti (1990) recounts an event that shook the world of the pure mathematicians during the early 1900's. David Hilbert attempting to purify mathematics of the sort of self-referential paradoxes that appear in ordinary language and logic [i.e. "The village barber shaves all those in the village who do not shave themselves. Who shaves the barber? (p.361)] proposed that it was possible to prove that the solution to every mathematical problem was either true or impossible. Shortly thereafter, Kurt Godel published his Incompleteness Theorem, an event which permanently ended Hilbert's and others' quest for a means of formalizing all mathematical truths. In effect, the implication of Godel's Theorem was to show that what is true and what is provable are not the same things.

Stripped to its bare essentials, what Godel's Theorem accomplished was to shatter forever the belief that there is no difference between truth and proof. The theorem's punch line is that there is an eternally unbridgeable gap between what's true (and can even be seen to be true) within a given logical framework or system and what we can actually prove by logical means using that same system. (p.328). Many, including Casti, regard the result of Godel's Theorem as the most profound and far-ranging philosophical result of the century.

Several perhaps, but not all or even most teachers sense the impact of Godel's work on their teaching. Betty Sonnet would be the first to admit that they don't get into proving things in the English department and that incompleteness is basically what most writing assignments are given for a grade. In his physics lab, Joe Galvanometer has enough trouble getting across empirical truths and is perfectly willing to leave that axiomatic stuff up to the math department. Whatever, in reality, it is that a mathematical proof proves, does not concern him. He believes in the existence of falling objects and sound waves but rarely questions what sort of an existence parabolas or sine curves have on their own. That kind of reality, he assumes is intuitively obvious, at least enough so it can be used.

Actually, Joe is partially right. The concept of intuition is basic to at least two schools of mathematical philosophy. Casti (1990) offers a summary of the four main positions on what's objectively real in mathematics (pp. 394-400). These are formalism, logicism, intuitionism, and Platonism. Platonism refers to "the shadows on the wall of a cave, shadows cast by ideal, abstract objects inhabiting a universe outside ordinary time and space" (p.396). Godel would be considered a Platonist holding, for example, that the Pythagorean Theorem applies to an ideal triangle which exists in the Platonic realm. "The reality of this ideal triangle is just as real as the physicist's quark or the sociobiologist's 'selfish gene'" (p.396). Contact with this shadowed realm of ideal, abstract objects, according to Godel, is made possible by the development of a sense of mathematical intuition.

Contemplating what math is all about, being aware, appreciative, and perhaps more sensitive to what math can both do and not do, the unsettled math teacher may now harbor some heavy questions about this subject that 1) operates from the premise that what's true and what's provable are not the same things at all , and 2) does not profess to say anything about the existence or reality of things. If not truth, then what do proofs prove? If not the reality of things, then the reality of what? What is the reality of mathematics? Indeed, Bertrand Russell may have been right when he said that "pure mathematics is the subject in which we do not know what we are talking about, or whether what we are saying is true" (Casti, p.365).

Taking a cue from his friends in physics, the undaunted math teacher observes the empirical data before him. Behold, there are three textbooks; copies of the teacher's editions (with answers) of Algebra 1, Geometry, and Algebra 2 with Trigonometry. Hardly, he thinks, do these comprise pure math. If they did, listings of all true answers in the backs of the books wouldn't exist, much less solution manuals. Correct answers are provided in these books, hence these books are not purely about pure math. Not overly impressed with his flawed logic, the resolved math teacher does, nevertheless, conclude that proofs prove mathematical truths and that mathematics has a reality of its own.

Once again more comfortable with his choice of profession, the math teacher nevertheless realizes that he has chosen a rather special discipline to teach. The mysteries, the unresolved problems, the occasional surprises, the challenges of creatively adapting to novel situations, and the forces of intrigue that motivate the mathematicians who generate mathematics are at the heart of his subject. What about these will he try to teach? Surely, he will teach the rules, the processes, and the algorithms in whatever way he can because to get beyond, they must be learned.. Beyond them, though, is mathematics. Will he, in fact, try to teach mathematics? Merely to accept that challenge may be the difference between being a good or a mediocre math teacher.

The next time you see Bob he says to you, "I thought you were going to explain your de-stuffing math problem and what you had learned about it."

"Its an open ended problem," you say ceremoniously. "The solution I expect to see alters, even creates the solution I do see. I am truly not sure what I have found. That's Heisenberg…. The Uncertainty Principle. It applies here."

"Since when did you become a quantum mechanic," Bob says.

"Since Liz threw me that monkey wrench."

RECESS
A tutor who tooted the flute
Tried to tutor two tooters to toot.
Said the two to the tutor:
Is it harder to toot, or
To tutor two tooters to toot

PART 9

"TC" Moss

Rather than de-stuffing math, you are learning the stuff of math and you are wondering why none of this has ever come up before. For you, math has always been factoring polynomials, solving for x, proving that tangents to a circle from the same point outside the circle are congruent, simplifying, rationalizing, trying, for heaven's sake, to show that you are almost as smart as the guy who put all those answers in the back of the book.

Math, you admit, will and must always be that. But aside from the problems in the text and the ones on the test, beside the SAT scores and the international comparisons; beyond the axioms, the numbers, the cool, abstract symbols, there are actually manifestations of real people that seem to have been ignored. There are the people who have made mathematics and the people who try to teach it. There are also the people who say how it should be taught and the people who say what should be taught. There are those who design and sell teaching materials for financial gain and those who exploit critical educational issues for political gain. Then, there are the parents who experience the consequences.

For your purposes, however, the person in the classroom is the one you want to key on. In your casual attempt to solve the problem of de-stuffing math, you learned much about the conditions that surround a math teacher but not much from the teacher's perspective. In the paper you prepared for the conference, you hit on some of the issues such as why some people end up teaching math and how they might feel about their subject, it being what it is. You recall thinking about being a math teacher yourself and you try to imagine what role you would be playing in a math department. That being too far fetched an idea to pursue you then think about Tom Brill and wonder what different roles will come his way over the years. You have heard the comment, how boring it must be to be a teacher and do the same things every day, year after year. You know it isn't that way but where in a career do the changes come about?

That's the question you put to Arne as you walk to the room where you will hold your workshop. Outside the door, a tall, overweight gentleman is standing. He is waiting for you. Arne tells you quickly that he is "TC" Moss, the State Superintendent for Mathematics Instruction. A hasty glance at your program tells you that a Dr. Theodore Cox Moss will be doing a workshop following yours in the same room. Seeing Arne, Dr. Moss waves and comes forward to say hello. Arne introduces you which brings forth a wide smile from Dr. Moss. "So you are the token parent," he says laughing.

He is a big, warm, totally relaxed man who seems to know everyone on a first name basis and who is known by everyone as "TC." He promises to come to my workshop if I come to his. Actually, we have no choice. "It seems," he says, "we are discussing complementary themes and Liz thought it would be interesting if we made a joint presentation. I'm game if you are."

Out of the corner of your eye, down the hall, you see a blue beret talking to Tim Gage and Dr. Stanley Miller. "Of course," you say, "I am honored." The sudden reorientation of events does have a short lived shock effect but you are relieved to have someone such as "TC" share the spotlight with you. You feel absolutely confident that he could and probably will make a star out of you.

"I have your notes," he says. "As a matter of fact, at coffee this morning when Liz told me about doing this with you, she gave me a copy. I have read them and I think we'll do just fine."

You see a mostly filled room as you enter. "You draw a nice crowd," you say.

The format of the workshop is simple. The papers you and "TC" have written aren't read. They form, rather, the basis for your remarks and the two of you have an informal dialogue referring to them as necessary. "TC" is masterful about giving you leading questions and rescuing you from lulls and the occasional lapse of memory. Since neither of you is advising the teachers what they should be doing or informing them about the latest new program that promises to improve their effectiveness, they don't have many questions to ask.

The workshop is over and you and "TC" make a few closing comments then stand. This is usually the moment when everyone gets up, starts talking loudly, checks programs to see where to go next, and moves toward the door. Not this time! Most of them remain seated as if alone in their thoughts. Then one or two rise, nod appreciatively in your direction, and leave quietly. Others follow.

"I am assuming they are thinking thoughtfully about what we said," he says.

As you leave, "TC" gives you a copy of his notes. Apparently Liz is having them all printed up and bound as an official record of the conference. You say good-bye and head off in opposite directions. You find a comfortable chair in the lobby and sit down. Another round of workshops has started. Except for the people at the reception table, the room is empty. Now what, you ponder, was "TC" saying about Stage 4 teachers not being distracted by dualism? You take his notes out of the brown envelope and start reading.

Without submitting to the formality of Piagetian stage criteria, it does seem reasonable to assert that teachers pass through a few identifiable stages of professional involvement during their careers. At least some generalized criteria noted by Gibbs (1978) can be identified in a teaching career. There appears to be a consecutive sequence of consistent interrelated developmental phases, a manifestation of upward directional mobility, and an assisted development in a socially fruitful environment. Assuming the existence of such stages, it may behoove math teachers to examine their surroundings and actions for clues as to where they stand and how they are handling it.

A personal library, in some way, reflects a teacher's stage of professional involvement. For example, a shelf of familiar college textbooks, well-worn binders of class notes to fall back on, and one uncracked edition of an algebra 1 text from, say, the latest series, *MATH 2000* published by Paradigm, Pageant, and Pixel: Boston, clearly identifies a Stage 1 math teacher.

Stage 1 math teachers are largely concerned with the mechanics, the logistics, and the concrete aspects of the act of teaching math rather than teaching. A 900 page text and 180 teaching days means 5 pages per day. Whether it is possible to cover 5 pp./d and what, in fact, is in all those pages is not the immediate consideration. Right answers are concrete evidence of student achievement and perceptive student observations verify good teaching. Call on the bright kids. Don't be distracted. Hold to the lesson plan. The exam counts 25% of the term grade. When signing reports, use a ball point pen and press hard. The second copy goes to the office.

Further, to Stage 1 teachers, objectives and operational procedures of educational methods and practices are taken literally. The precision in which these are performed may appear as important as their instructional outcomes. Skill in setting up and dismantling group activities or in conducting demonstrations, i.e. making certain abstract concepts real, may take precedence over the appropriateness of the chosen group activity or concept demonstrated. Social and professional perspectives tend to be compartmentalized perhaps for the sake of simplicity.

When the teachers' personal library starts filling up with textbooks of other publishing houses, freebies from regional and NCTM conferences, and the old college stuff gets put away, Stage 2 has arrived. Several texts are examined, cross referenced, and used to make up tests. Stage 2 teachers speak knowingly and critically about the subtle advantages and woeful omissions of this series as opposed to that. With expanded professional resources, improved teaching techniques, cutting edge computer skills, numerous admirers among the student body, growing friendships within the department, and a "can do" reputation with the administration, Stage 2 teachers are well aware of their developing talents. They find enjoyment in every aspect of teaching and feel secure in their chosen profession.

Rather than mastering the concrete acts of teaching, Stage 2 math teachers are attracted by the full capacities of being a teacher. They value recognition and symbols of achievement. They assume a sense of professional responsibility toward their own ambitions and become aware of related pragmatic needs. Among these may be the need to specialize, acquire an advanced degree, change schools, hold a leadership position in a local professional association, and serve on various school evaluation visiting committees. Stage 2 math teachers are professionally motivated.

One of the diagnostic characteristics of Stage 3 math teachers is a decrease in the number of high school textbooks on the shelf. Only a few of the tried and proven ones remain. Instead, there are books, more detailed and sophisticated, on specific topics such as mappings, tessellations, sequences, symmetry, fractals, topology, logic, and non-Euclidean geometries. In addition, there is a growing, ordered collection of professional journals, computer updates, plus a variety of books reflecting personal interests in, perhaps, cosmology, environmental science, or business cycles. Stage 3 math teachers continue to be teacher oriented and involved in the politics of different associations of mathematics. When their state or regional mathematics association is hosting an NCTM conference, they may serve as a facilitator or committee member. They have a greater sense of a community of math teachers than Stage 2 teachers and savor establishing mutual respect and sharing intrapersonal values with their colleagues. Also, they are generally more accepting of new ideas and seldom feel threatened by proposed changes. In a pinch, however, they fall back on the wisdom of their experiences.

Confident of professional support from their superiors, Stage 3 math teachers feel free to explore and develop their creative capabilities. They like to design new units, deviate from the regimentation of the text, and prefer to make up their own work sheets and tests. They experiment with alternative forms of assessment and extended group activities. Student rapport is built on the respect generated by shared involvement in learning situations. In Stage 3, time becomes less linear and lesson plans may be but sketchy outlines of undefined duration.

While experiencing confidence, freedom, and productivity, there comes as well a discontinuity at the outer edge of Stage 3. Essentially, it is a career based urge to stand apart, take stock, see the future all the way to the end. It is a moment perceived as the point of decision where the choices are move up, move on, or move out.

To move up generally means to become an administrator. Administrators have an office of their own if not a whole school. They make more money. They deal with broader issues and bigger people. They are seen as having been promoted to a higher, more prestigious position with greater responsibilities. They have the image of success. Further, skillful administrators can be the inspiration and the catalyst to make good things happen for many people. Administrators are selected for their insights, skills and resources. To be appointed and move up is a social and professional reaffirmation of extraordinary achievements. To be passed over can be a bummer.

On the other hand, becoming an administrator is to move out of the classroom and into the stressful arena of endless, answerless problems. To move on about your business as a math teacher may be the right decision. After all, the essence of education is a teacher and a student. The log thing. An administrator may be able to bring in another log, another student, and maybe exchange the logs for desks and put a roof over the desks. That's his job. Teachers teach and talented teachers are a vital national resource. If getting to be a talented teacher was the original motivation, stay put unless, in retrospect, the whole thing was a mistake. Stage 3 math teachers deciding to move on with their teaching careers are making personal reaffirmations of their commitment to become effective and inspiring teachers of mathematics.

Chalk it up to "burn out." Some teachers want to get away from students, classrooms, overly involved parents, administrators, schools, the whole bit. Tired of bringing papers home to grade every night, filling up weekends with workshops on the latest technical fad, attending special events on Friday nights, showing school spirit at the games on Saturday, working summers to make ends meet, their battle cry may be "get a life."

Math teachers who decide to move out are of two types, those who physically depart this teaching world and those who spiritually opt out. The former are gone. Good luck! The latter remain in body, waiting for social security to kick in or quietly riding out the job into which they have paid their dues. They assume the role of passive master doing only what they are known for doing best. They attend to their reputations and hearken to their intuitions within rather than to the actuality around them. In short, they "wing it." This is unfortunate but not all bad. If, like a small, light aircraft, they are capable of a long, powerless glide, they could be used effectively by a savvy administrator. If, on the other hand, they are more like a helicopter, they would do well to abandon any ideas of winging it.

Math teachers having successfully made this quantum leap into Stage 4, may observe that their professional library is becoming indistinguishable from the rest of the library. The well used and still relevant and reliable books remain but among them may be fiction and poetry and travel books. Tall art books lean to accommodate the shelf space. Books on gardening and birds are as handy as those on calculus and discrete math. It might be said that things are coming together.

Stage 4 math teachers seem to have developed a unified personal philosophy about their lives and their profession. Dualism's no longer distract them. The either/or of means/end, objective/subjective, individual/society, teacher/student, cowboy/Indian, whatever, exist but need not necessarily be compartmentally defended/attacked, as it were. The means to attain a better grade is the grade earned. The individual student is the student body. The teacher is always the student. Godel might have to back him up but even fact can be fiction. The professional interests of Stage 4 math teachers, therefore, tend to be broad in scope and multidimensional. Process is more intriguing than result and pattern more fascinating than detail.

To some of their colleagues, Stage 4 math teachers may appear to be dreamers, in a world of their own, dispensing more anecdotes than formulas. This is a mistake. Stage 4 math teachers can be very effective in the classroom and extremely efficient. They seem to know precisely where the student is and what he or she needs next to move on. Having a broad overview of their subject, they can produce that need no matter where it may occur in the agenda of the text. Stage 4 math teachers can go through a unit in non-linear form, incorporating discrete ideas, relevant yarns, and open ended questions then, at the right moment, bring everything into brilliant focus with maximum impact.

It is easy to associate these four stages with ages but this does not necessarily hold. It is also natural to think that each stage is an improvement over the preceding one. As a matter of fact, each stage has a unique height to which it alone can ascend. They are not to be qualitatively compared. Taken together, they are a complete sequence. Into their careers, math teachers may wonder at what stage have they arrived. Answering this, a Stage 4 math teacher might comment "where individual teachers would like to be is probably where they are."

Partly because it exists, though with few legitimate members, and partly to allow Stage 4 teachers to satisfy the upward directional mobility criteria, a Stage 5 must be recognized. More than a level where teachers would like to be, it is that stage to which some math teachers unintentionally progress. Having left the classroom, they still teach in the abstract, making up new problems and solving old ones.

In Stage 5, there are both math teachers and mathematicians. There are musicians and artists and all those whose life-long careers became to them, at some point, a passion, a purpose for being . It is often a solitary position. In his superb biography of Einstein, Pais (1982) gives Einstein's own description of his closing years.

> 'I have become an obstinate heretic in the eyes of my colleagues,' he wrote to one friend, and to another, 'I am generally regarded as a sort of petrified object, rendered blind and deaf by the years. I find this role not too distasteful, as it corresponds very well with my temperament.' He knew and on occasion would even say, that his road was a lonely one, yet he held fast. 'Momentary success carries more power of conviction for most people than reflections on principles.' (p. 462)

Having finished reading the notes that "TC" gave you, you put them back in the envelope and walk down the corridor into the crowd of math teachers who are noisily moving to their next meeting. You have always thought of math teachers as being alone in a classroom. You have never experienced a mass of them all together. In a strange way, having no identifiable stage of your own, you feel like an imposter.

RECESS

Oh. The grand old Duke of York,
He had ten thousand men,
He marched them up to the top of the hill,
And he marched them down again.
And when they were up they were up,
And when they were down they were down,
And when they were only half way up,
They were neither up nor down.

PART 10

▼

DAVE ELLERT

The conference day is half over. Your plan is to hear the lady talk about "Hands On Math" and then catch some lunch. Just as you are about to enter the room a man behind you says, "How can you have hands on abstractions?" You turn and playfully counter with "much less the Uncertainties." He smiles and says, "Heisenberg! Hey that's pretty good."

Not quite attuned to math teacher humor you say pompously, "Hands on is using blocks and tiles and tapes and balancing devices to help make the transition from concrete models to symbolic thinking."

"Ho-wah!" he yells out. "Now none of us will have to go in." The disapproving glances you get from those around you clearly suggest that going in now might not be such a hot idea. "Come on," he says, "I'll buy you a coffee."

The snack bar is just off the lobby. You get your coffee and sit at a little round table near a window looking out into the lobby. Liz is out there clearing off the tables, sorting unused materials, and setting up a box to collect the Conference Evaluation Forms. Your new friend joins you. His WELCOME sticker, you note, has Dave Ellert printed on it. He checks yours out. So much for introductions.

Dave, you sense, is very bright and given to cynicism. He has taught at the same urban school for twenty years and for that precise amount of time has shared departmental duties with eight idiots (Ho-wah!) teaching everything from "pre-math" (his term) to BC Calculus. His students are "dumber than dirt" and "the administrators haven't had an original thought since they were toilet trained." Experience has taught you never to ask such people why they stay where they are.

"I'm not a teacher of mathematics," you confess.

"That's all right, neither are most of the people here. At least you are honest about it."

"No, really. I'm a parent," you say and then add hurriedly to cut off a possible ho-wah, "I was asked to give a little presentation."

"So you are an impostor too," he says. "I'm supposed to be a history teacher."

Dave then goes on to tell you how he was hired to teach American history and government but just before school was to open the math chairman had a mild stroke. In that none of the other math teachers could handle the advanced courses and he being right out Williams and all, the principal asked him if he would teach a little math for a while. Dave agreed, secretly admitting how relieved he was not to have to teach the Civil War. As a matter of fact, he liked the cool, impersonal, rigor, of math so much that by February he had lined up a summer graduate program that ultimately got him properly certified to teach middle and high school math.

"Ho-wah," you venture.

You then tell him about the steps you have taken to find an answer to the question "When am I ever going to use this stuff?" He is particularly complimentary of Tom Brill's historical approach and Tim Gage's attempts to find both constructive and truthful ways to assess student achievement in mathematics. However, he is most intrigued by Bob Willard's view that the preparation for and the teaching of mathematics is a unique and almost isolated experience.

"Right on," he says. "The true teacher of mathematics may never be understood and without a better knowledge of what that teacher is trying to do, he can hardly be appreciated. As far as de-stuffing math is concerned, it would be easier to de-sand all the beaches in the world."

"But not impossible," you say. "Gauss didn't have to deal with math stuff."

"Gauss was a mathematician, not a math teacher."

"Then it's the math teachers who generate or attract math stuff?"

"I don't know about that," Dave says, "but the industry they are involved in is big business. There is plenty in it to keep people confused. Like politics. Every four years somebody wants to cash in on the promise that he will be 'the education president.' Every two years somebody points to the leaks in the school roof, the over crowding, and the need for tougher standards. Fortunately for them the leaks are still available issues two years later. Between election years you hear about fiscal responsibility and budgetary restraint in light of the proposed revenue producing Convention Center. While all this is going on, you have taught the Fundamental Theorem of Algebra four times."

"Isn't that being a little hard on politicians?"

"Don't go soft on me," he says. "What I'm saying is that politicians, school boards and the like are involved in their own agendas. At best, they can only slightly and incidentally bring about changes in the way math is taught. Those changes can be either positive or negative. In spite of their hype though, these people are not the force that will make lasting improvements in the teaching of math."

"In my district, the school board is adding two days to the school year. That's two more math periods. Won't that help?"

Dave laughs. "That's a two day extension to the 'senior slump.' Oh, I suppose that if you think of one of those days as being in November when you are struggling with trig and the other in February when you are trying to teach convergent sequences it might help."

"Well, how about the new textbooks and teaching materials and calculators and those fancy graphing utilities?"

"Now you are talking big business. The stuff you just mentioned adds up to about two hundred bucks per student. Somebody is making out all right. But that's OK. Its marketing and, like politics, its part of the process, just another force that possibly could influence the way math is taught."

Dave leaves the question hanging so you have to you ask, "Does it help? Is the marketing, the publishing, whatever, effective as a force to improve the situation?"

"Change the situation? Yes! Improve it? That depends on how good or bad the previously used materials were. Some of the best books I have seen were used in the 60's. A few of the latest ones are also excellent. I would have to say that, like politicians, the producers of educational materials have the power to insert changes in the process that can keep the pressure on to improve the teaching of math, but make major changes by themselves, no way."

Whether he is correct or not, Dave has a strong opinion about everything. For instance, he regards some school administrators as being part of a massive inert system frozen by a fear of public criticism. The educational psychologists and theorists who conduct studies and write books, on the other hand, are the poets who offer visionary choices and directions to explore. They are not, and don't pretend to be, the generals who move mountains. The National Councils and Foundations that set standards, the ETS, the ACT, and all the people who design and sell tests can and do effect both the what and the way math is taught in rigid but not necessarily profound ways."

"Look Dave," you say, "we're not getting very far with the 'how to improve the teaching of math' problem. You've eliminated or declared weak every possible force so far. There is only one left and I'll bet it's the teacher. The teacher is the primary means through which positive measures can be taken. Right?"

"I'll give you a C+ for that," Dave says. "The teacher being in the classroom where changes take place may be a means but as a force, the teacher is the weakest."

"The weakest? All those stories and movies about great teachers and how they brought about remarkable changes in their students, weren't they documenting the power of teaching?"

"The teacher is like gravity," Dave says. "Everybody can see the apple fall out of the tree and everybody can see how Suzy has improved since being in your geometry class but being obvious doesn't mean being strong. In this case it means being local, on the spot. Beyond the classroom, the inspiring teaching isn't heard. Beyond the earth, the apple is on its own."

You think of Ennis Ryan and his efforts to change the way geometry is taught or at least change the sequence in which geometry is taught. And then there is Tom Brill who is trying to humanize math by introducing math history. In each case, the effort is indeed local and you wonder how long these teachers will be able to sustain their interests. Perhaps to support them you say, "OK, assuming you are right, finding the means is enough for now. Let's build on that. How can we pump up the teacher?"

"Ah, the poor teacher of mathematics." Dave says tenderly. "Do you know what an ellipsoid is?"

"Not in this context," you say, slightly irritated at the sudden digression.

"An ellipsoid is a closed, positively curved surface. It is like a sphere only it is shaped more like a football. It is far more complex than the two dimensional, flat plane that most of us think on. For one thing, there are no straight lines, no clear right or wrong directions, much less pie charts and bar graphs to display our simple findings. There are ellipses that crisscross over the surface like the great and small circles that bound the earth. A point on the ellipsoid is called an elliptic point because calling it merely a point is inadequate. On the earth, there is the 'polar' point. It has two parts, a north part and a south part. The same goes for the elliptic point. Somewhere each has a counter part.

"I don't have the slightest idea what you are talking about," you say looking dreamily through the window. Liz's mindless tasks, nearly completed, seem strangely appealing suddenly. "What's all this got to do with the poor teacher of mathematics?"

"I see those special teachers thinking and working in an elliptical environment. They are points on an ellipsoid. Intersecting over their heads are the many ellipses of the politicians, the test makers, the publishers, the administrators, the standard setters, the educational theorists, each with counter points of view of their own which declare when and how the teachers of mathematics should work in the essentials of six years of math into four."

"Dave," you say, "You're weird."

Dave re-groups himself. "There is, as Yogi Berra might have said, more to being a math teacher than being a math teacher. Or, the sum of its parts is more than the whole"

"Actually," you say, "I do know what you mean. In my role as surrogate math teacher, I have become aware of and sensitive to some of a math teacher's unique problems and suspect that I may have contributed to one of them."

"You mean I should have included an ellipse for you too?"

"Well, I have gathered that of all the high school subjects mathematics is, perhaps, the least understood and most weakly defended. For example, as a parent of a student having troubles with math, I now regretfully recall the times I apathetically said that I never really understood math either. The fact that I have now happily mastered adulthood seems to reinforce the notion that an apparent lack of math skills doesn't much matter anyway. 'Math is good for mathematicians,' they say. 'For the rest, however, mathematics beyond the calculator simply doesn't exist.' Relative to the math I learned and still remember, they may be right about that."

Dave softens his tone. "The kind and amount of math that is remembered partly depends on how often math is used. The longevity of math or any subject is 'at risk' if the content of that subject figures minimally in the daily routine. In math, for most people, other than adding, subtracting and occasionally multiplying, rarely dividing, are 'math thoughts' entertained on a day to day basis. In fact, as a used tool, math undoubtedly rates well below the automobile, the ball point pen, and the garden rake. In the area of recreation, beyond golf and tennis and season tickets, people do read books, attend lectures and concerts, visit art and science museums, and tour historic sights. However, I don't suspect for most people there is much entertainment value in real mathematics."

Recalling Susan Langer's view, that math deals with irrelevant sensory qualities and professes nothing about the existence of things, you have little wonder as to why recreational math is not a big item. Yet, you think, if the majority of people were like Fibonacci, Viete, and Euler, someone probably would have designed a math theme park by now.

"Anyway," Dave says perking up, "you aren't the problem. The problem that American educators face today is not about adult proficiency in math. It is about student achievement in math at certain selected grade levels. The results of the Second and now the Third International Mathematics and Science Study released in 1998 of student achievement throughout the world, thoughtfully displayed on a bar graph so everybody can interpret them, show that the bar over the United States is pretty anemic. Many other national tests given by the states show the same thing. The problem seems to be that our kids aren't learning math well at all."

"Isn't that just what we have been talking about?"

"Yeah, only now its official. Everybody will be trying to figure out the problem. Each of those ellipses that converge on the elliptic point of the teacher has a vested interest not only in the problem but also in the solution they put forth."

"I suppose," you say, "charter schools and vouchers are examples of politically conservative solutions. The standards crowd seems to be basing its solution on a notion of fixed accountability that assumes the existence of unproved equalities. One can only imagine the array of solutions offered by the test makers, the marketers, the Boards of Education, and the national councils. Believe it or not, that ellipsoid of yours is beginning to come into focus."

Dave goes on as if he had just made a study of the problem. "Explanations for the poor showing," he says, "seems to range from the defensive to the constructive. It has been suggested that: the test didn't fairly represent the American syllabus; that some nations had greater control over which of their students would participate; that our math curriculum is at fault, that our textbooks are too long; that either our school day or school year or both is too short; that our students are too involved in non-academic activities; that our program suffers by being compartmentalized; that the expressive teaching methods and group learning are too unfocused; that instructive methods and rote learning weaken incentive; and that we don't teach math in sufficient depth."

"On the other hand," he continues, "it has not been widely noted that the number of hours math teachers spend "off task" (not teaching or preparing) is inversely proportional to students' scores. Nor has it been suggested that if math teachers earned an income competitive with other professions, many of those highly talented people who now become chemists and engineers and doctors would have another economically viable option to consider upon graduation. Some feel that our schools of education should figure out what it is that they are supposed to do and do it. Sadly however, in the final analysis, the low scores will probably be blamed on poor teaching."

"Unfortunately, poor teaching carries with it the implication of poor teachers. One explanation I read said that our curriculum by comparison consists of 'low quality content' and that the material we teach is not sufficiently 'substantial.' Further, our teaching methods and techniques were questioned. Apparently, they video taped classes from all over and observed that American math teachers were, among other things, lacking in bringing their lessons to a wrap-up, summary, closing point. In their defense, the Americans say that they were spending too much time trying to prep for external tests and adjust to new and often conflicting standards. Another factor suggested is that athletics and activities require far more student time and energy in America than elsewhere. Whatever, the situation isn't good and the ellipses overhead are humming with solutions."

"It sounds like we are facing a serious crisis," you say, "doubly so since we appear to have no strong and reliable forces to bring about the necessary changes." In the silence that follows, it occurs to you that either your math stuff issue, along with math teaching in general, has become completely unraveled or else Dave Ellert is a skilled alarmist. For immediate reassurance, you check to see if Liz has restored order to the conference table out in the lobby. To your relief, she has and you hope there is something symbolic about it. Not only that but she is still wearing a 'blue' beret which, Becky has told you, signifies 'control.' "Hang in there Liz," you mutter.

Dave is showing a different expression. "You know what?" he says.

"At this point," you say, "I can guarantee that I do not know what."

He leans forward and says, "I don't think that there will be a significant change in the way math is taught in this country for some time. Improving public education may be a useful political issue but the issue is not being clearly defined and that is because the voters prefer it that way. They want diversity; vouchers for private tuition, home schooling, chartered schools, all that. They are not saying that the Jeffersonian ideal for public education is wrong.

They just don't want to talk about it. The principle is fine, they just aren't too excited about paying for somebody else's education. Individualism reigns; communal concerns like strong public schools are secondary. Let's face it, the whole institution of public education, at this time in history, is being eroded. When the culture of the country encourages this or even just lets it happen, there isn't much of a chance for serious changes to succeed."

"I get it," you say. "The existing national culture is the key force. Come to think about it, I doubt if the people today would support a Marshall Plan or be willing to finance a GI Bill sort of program or spend public money re-educating teachers like the National Science Foundation fellowships of the 50's and 60's."

"Exactly," Dave says. "Look at the contrasting moods of the country toward two, so called, non-core areas, athletics and the arts. One is heavily financed and always forgiven for it numerous transgressions. The other is begrudgingly financed and forever held accountable for a few violations of mass artistic taste. If low math scores should someday offend the national mood, by the same token, math teachers' pay could be reduced and certain areas of the curriculum could be banned. Why not?"

"Elliptically speaking," you say with mock seriousness, "that could happen. But on a bar graph, hardly."

Dave is pleased with your response like a teacher might be suddenly hearing a student come up with an insightful comment. "You pass," he says.

You were joking. The connection escapes you but at this point you are willing to let it go. "Dave, we have math teaching in the dark ages. I don't suppose there are a few monasteries around to keep the flame of Pythagoras going."

"As a matter of fact," he says, "we do, although I don't imagine they would like to be thought of that way. There is in this country a group of well focused, philosophically and pedagogically sound private schools. Actually, they prefer to be called independent schools and for the most part are members of the highly esteemed National Association of Independent Schools. Rather than compete with, or profit from the weaknesses of public education, the independent schools augment the national system. In some ways they are experimental and in other ways they maintain and upgrade proven traditions. They have high, self imposed standards and are quite capable of moving the model of a wise and enlightened educational system forward."

"Are there any public school monasteries?" you ask.

"I don't think you'll find monasteries in the public school system but it's possible," Dave says. "Rather than quiet little schools doing their thing, there are several bold high schools that specialize in something like math or science. I'd say they are more like cathedrals than monasteries. There are also some excellent schools often associated with or close to a university that maintain high ideals and standards."

"The model is safe, then. When do you think we can get back to the real thing, the Full Monty?"

Dave goes oblique on you again. "Right after Bunker Hill, Fort Sumter, Black Tuesday, Pearl Harbor. Right after something like that. At least that. Whatever."

"A crisis?" you ask. "Do you mean a major crisis?"

Dave's answer is interrupted by a sudden rush of math teachers starting to fill the lobby. Some are checking the bulletin board for messages, some perusing Liz's table for possible freebies, and others are heading for the snack bar. Dave hurriedly gets up. "Think I'll catch another session," he says. "Its either *Games For Your Graphing Utility* or *Integrating Math And Recess.* What do you think?"

"Dave," you say, "you're one sick history teacher."

"See you, fellow impostor," he says smiling.

As you walk out into the lobby, you watch Dave disappear among those leaving and entering the session rooms. Towering over a small group of teachers you see TC laughing and waving his arms in friendly conversation. If he knows anything about an impending crisis, he is certainly keeping it concealed. You look up at the large glass dome above the lobby. Supporting beams rising up toward its center seem to cross over your head. Are they great circles or ellipses and are you at an elliptic point?

You are well aware that with or without you the math teachers will move on in discrete groups from meeting to meeting where they will hear about the new math series and the newer math series, the axiomatic approach, the concrete approach, the algebraic approach to whatever, and the ever rejuvenated spiral curriculum whose novelty this year is to go counter-clockwise. By tomorrow, they all will have returned to their schools and to the secure familiarity of their own classrooms. Having heard what they should be teaching and how they should teach it, the math teachers are left with the mundane decisions of whether to start trig after spring break but before reviewing for the SAT's or to cut statistics and start trig now, hoping not all of their students are in the up-coming production of West Side Story. You recall, with some embarrassment, your grandiose thoughts on those who chose to become math teachers and how manageable it all seemed, once reconciled to Godel's Incompleteness Theorem.. The vision of all this, the possible external pressures of politicians and those whose market is education, plus the amorphous force of the national will, depict a reality far too complex to be analyzed on a two dimensional bar graph. You entered the select realm of the teachers of mathematics seeking their help and understanding. In your quest for a simple answer to the question "When will I ever use this stuff," you found instead the elliptic universe of the math teacher.

References and Bibliography

Suggested Math and Science Books Listed By Title

A Dictionary of Mathematics, John Glenn and Graham Littler, Editors. New York: Harper and Row, 1984.

A Brief History of Time, Stephen W. Hawking. New York: Bantam, 1988.

A History of Mathematics, Second Edition, Carl B. Boyer and Uta C. Merzbach. New York: Wiley and Sons, Inc. 1989.

Automata Networks in Computer Science, Francoise Fogelman Soulie, Yves Robert and Maurice Tchuente, Editors. Princeton: Princeton University Press, 1987.

Cellular Automata Machines, A New Environment for Modeling, Tommaso Toffoli and Norman Margolus. Cambridge, MA: The MIT Press, 1987.

Chaos, Making a New Science, James Gleick. New York: Viking, 1987.

Exploring the Geometry of Nature, Edward Rietman. Blue Ridge Summit, PA: Windcrest Books, 1989.

Fermat's Last Theorem, Amir D. Aczel. New York: Dell Publishing, 1997.

Fire In The Mind; Science, Faith, and the Search For Order, George Johnson. New York: Alfred A. Knopf, 1995.

Fractal Mania, Phil Laplante. New York: Windcrest/McGraw-Hill, 1994.

Fractals For The Classroom, Heinz-Otto Peitgen, Hartmut Jurgens, .
      Dietmar Saupe. New York: Springer-Verlag, in cooperation with
      the NCTM, 1992 (Corrected second printing, 1993).

Game, Set and Math, Enigmas and Conundrums, Ian Stewart. New York:
      Viking Penguin, 1989.

Godel, Escher, Bach: An Eternal Golden Braid, Douglas R. Hofstader. New
      York: Basic Books, 1979.

Mind Tools, Rudy Rucker. Boston: Houghton Mifflin, 1987.

Parallel Universes, Fred Alan Wolf. New York: Simon and Schuster, 1988.

Poetry of the Universe, Robert Osserman. New York: Anchor Books, 1995.

Relativity Visualized, Lewis Carroll Epstein. San Francisco: Insight Press,
      1981.

Science of Chaos, Christopher Lampton. New York: Venture, 1992.

Taking the Quantum Leap, Fred Alan Wolf. San Francisco: Harper & Row,
      1981.

The Art of Mathematics, Jerry P. King. New York: Fawcett Columbine,
      1992.

The Emperor's New Mind, Roger Penrose. Oxford, UK: Oxford
      University Press, 1989. Also Penguin Books, 1991.

The End of Time, Julian Barbour. New York: Oxford University Press,
      1999.

The Fractal Geometry of Nature, Benoit B. Mandelbrot. San Francisco: W.
      H. Freeman, 1983.

The History of Mathematics, Roger Cooke. New York: John Wiley & Sons,
      1997.

The Science of Fractal Images, M.F. Barnsley, R.L. Devaney, B.B.
      Mandelbrot, H.-O. Peitgen, D.Saupe. R,F. Voss. Heinz-Otto Peitgen
      and Dietmar Saupe, Editors. New York: Springer-Verag, 1988.

The User Illusion, Tor Norretranders. New York: Viking., 1991.

The VNR Concise Encyclopedia of Mathematics, W.Gellert, H.Kustner,
      M.Hellwich, and H.Kastner, Editors. New York: Van Nostrand
      Reinhold, 1977.

Who Got Einstein's Office?, Ed Regis. Reading, MA: Addison-Wesley, 1987.
Zero To Lazy Eight, Alexander Humez, Nicholas Humez and Joseph
    Maguire. New York: Touchstone Books/Simon and Schuster, 1993.

Bibliography Including References for DR. Miller's Lecture

Armstrong, Thomas (1994). *Multiple Intelligences in the Classroom.*
    Alexandria, Virginia: Association for Supervision and Development.
Bailey, James (1996). *After Thought, The Computer Challenge to Human
    Intelligence.* New York, Basic Books.
Brandt, Ron (1989). On Cooperative Learning: A Conversation With
    Spencer Kagan. *Education Leadership. 47,* 8-11.
Brandt, Ron (1990). On Knowledge and Cognitive Skills: A Conversation
    With David Perkins. *Education Leadership. 47,* 50-53.
Capra, Fritjor (1982). *The Turning Point: Science, Society, And The Rising
    Culture.* New York: Bantam Books.
Casti, John L. (1990). *Searching For Certainty: What Scientists Can Know
    About The Future.* New York: William Morrow and Company, Inc.
Clarke, Barbara (1986). *Optimizing Learning: The Integrative Education
    Model in the Classroom.* Columbus Ohio: Merrill.
Core Standing Committee (1993). *Choosing Courses to Prepare for College.*
    Harvard University,:Cambridge, MA:: unpublished pamphlet.
DeBono, Edward (1970). *Lateral Thinking: Creativity Step By Step.* New
    York: Harper And Row.
E. Angus Powell Endowment for American Enterprise (1991). *Model
    School Curriculum for Economic Education for K-12.* Richmond,
    Virginia: E. Angus Powell Endowment.
Eisner, Elliot W. (1985). *The Art of Education Evaluation: A Personal View.*
    Philadelphia: Falmer Press.
Eisnew, Elliot W. (1991). What Really Counts in Schools. *Educational
    Leadership. 48,* 10-17.
Elkind, David (1986). Formal Education and Early Childhood
    Education: An Essential Difference. *Kappan. 67*(9), 631=636.

Ellis, Susan S. and Whalen, Susan F. (1990). *Cooperative Learning: Getting Started*. New York: Scholastic.

Gardner, Howard (1985). *Frames of Mind: The Theory of Multiple Intelligence*. New York: Basic Books.

Gardner, Howard (1991). *The Unschooled Mind: How Children Think and How Schools Should Teach*. New York: Basic Books.

Gardner, Howard (1993). *Multiple Intelligences: The Theory in Practice*. New York: Basic Books.

Gibbs, John C. (1978). Stage Theories of Cognitive and Moral Development: Criticisms and Applications. *Harvard Educational Review. Reprint No. 13,* 37-40.

Glasser, William M.D. (1992). *The Quality School: Managing Students Without Coercion,* (2nd expanded ed.). New York: Harper Perennial.

Goodlad, John I. (1984). *A Place Called School: Prospects For The Future*. New York: McGraw-Hill.

Hall, Edward T. (1959). *The Silent Language*. Greenwich, CT: Fawcett Publications, Inc.

Hawking, Stephen W. (1988). *A Brief History of Time: From The Big Bang To Black Holes*. New York: Bantam Books.

Heath, Douglas H. (1994). *Schools of Hope: Developing Mind and Character in Today's Youth*. San Francisco: Jossey-Bass.

Hendricks, Robert H, Nappi Andrew T., Dawson George G., Mattils, Mindy M. (1989). *Learning Economics Through Childrens Stories,* (5th ed.). New York: Joint Council on Economic Education.

Johnson, David W. and Johnson Roger T. (1993). Gifted Students Illustrate What Isn't Cooperative Learning. *Educational Leadership. 50,* 60-64.

Kagan, Spencer (1989). The Sytructural Approach to Cooperative Learning. *Educational Leadership. 47,* 12-15.

Kantrowitz, Barbara and Winert, Pat (1989). How Kids Learn, *Newsweek. 113,* 50-56.

Kohn, Alfie (1991). Don't Spoil the Promises of Cooperative Learning: Response to Slavin, *Educational Leadership. 48*, 93-94.

Krechevsky, Mara (1991). Project Spectrum: An Innovative Assessment Alternative. *Educational Leadership, 48*, 93-94.

Kutnick, Peter J. (1990). A Social Critique of Cognitively Based Science Curricular. Leopold E. Klopfer (Ed.). *Science Education* (87-94). New York: Wiley-Interscience.

Langer, Susanne K. (1942). *Philosophy In A New Key.* New York: Mentor Books.

Leinhardt, Gaea (1992). What Research on Learning Tells Us About Teaching. *Educational Leadership. 49*, 21-25.

Norrethanders, Tor (1991). *The User Illusion: Cutting Consciousness Down To Size.* New York: Viking.

Pais, Abraham (1982). *'Subtle is the Lord...' The Science and the Life of Albert Einstein.* Oxford, UK: Oxford University Press.

Pais, Abraham (1991). *Niels Bohr,s Times, In Physics, Philosophy, and Polity.* Oxford, UK: Oxford University Press.

Perkins, David (1992). *Smart Schools: Better Thinking and Learning for Every Child.* New York: The Free Press.

Peitgen, Heins-Otto, Harmut Jurgens, Dietmar Saupe (1992). *Fractals for the Classroom.* New York: Springer-Verlag, in cooperation with the NCTM (Corrected second printing, 1993.).

Perrone, Vito (ed.) (1991). *Expanding Student Assessment.* Alexandria, Virginia: Association for Supervision and Curriculum Development.

Pitcher, George (1971). *A Theory of Perception.* Princeton, NJ: Princeton University Press.

Regis, Ed (1987). *Who Got Einstein's Office?* Reading, MA: Addison-Wesley Publishing Company, Inc.

Rucker, Rudy (1987). *Mind Tools: The Five Levels of Mathematical Reality.* Boston: Houghton Mifflin Company.

Shanker, Albert (1995, March 19). Where We Stand: Beyond Magic Bullets. *New York Times, E,* 7.

Siegel, Janna and Shaughnessy, Michael F. (1994). An Interview With Howard Gardner: Educating for Understanding. *Kappan.* *75*(7), 563-566.

Sizer, Theodore R. (1992). *Horace's School: Redesigning the American High School.* New York: Houghton Mifflin Company.

Slavin, Robert E. (1989). Research on Cooperative Learning: Consensus and Controversy. *Educational Leadership.* *47*, 52-54.

Slavin, Robert E. (1991). Synthesis of Research on Cooperative Learning. *Educational Leadership.* *48*, 71-82.

Sternberg, Robert J, (1988). *The Triarchic MIND: a New Theory of Human Intelligence.* New York: Penguin Books.

Straus, William and Howe, Neil (1997). *The Fourth Turning: An American Prophecy.* New York: Broadway Books.

Wang, Hao (1987). *Reflections on Kurt Godel.* Cambridge, MA: The MIT Press.